EASY PIANO

Love Songs of the '80s & '90s

ISBN 0-7935-8344-6

HAL•LEONARD®
CORPORATION

7777 W. BLUEMOUND RD. P.O. BOX 13819 MILWAUKEE, WI 53213

For all works contained herein:
Unauthorized copying, arranging, adapting, recording or public performance is an infringement of copyright.
Infringers are liable under the law.

Visit Hal Leonard Online at
www.halleonard.com

WITHDRAWN

Love Songs of the '80s & '90s

Contents

ALL FOR LOVE

from Walt Disney Pictures' THE THREE MUSKETEERS

Words and Music by BRYAN ADAMS,
ROBERT JOHN "MUTT" LANGE and MICHAEL KAMEN

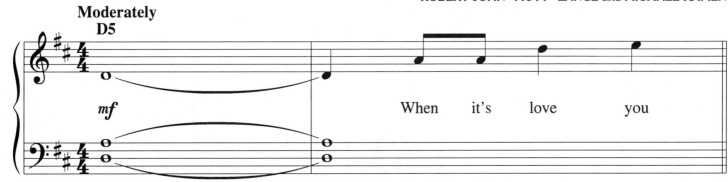

© 1993 Wonderland Music Company, Inc., Sony/ATV Songs LLC, K-Man Corp., Badams Music Ltd. and Zomba Enterprises Inc.
Wonderland Music Company, Inc., 500 S. Buena Vista Street, Burbank, CA 91521
All Rights on behalf of Sony/ATV Songs LLC, K-Man Corp. and Badams Music Ltd.
Administered by Sony/ATV Music Publishing, 8 Music Square West, Nashville, TN 37203
International Copyright Secured   All Rights Reserved

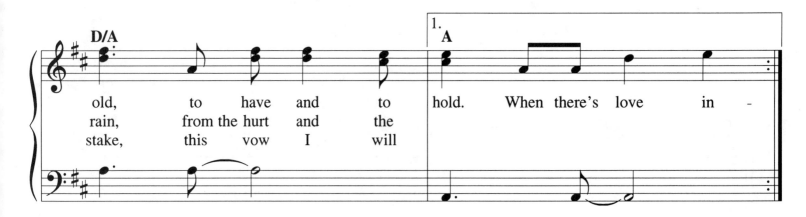

old,   to have and to hold. When there's love in -
rain,   from the hurt and the
stake,   this vow I will

pain.   Let's make it all for one and all for
make: that it's

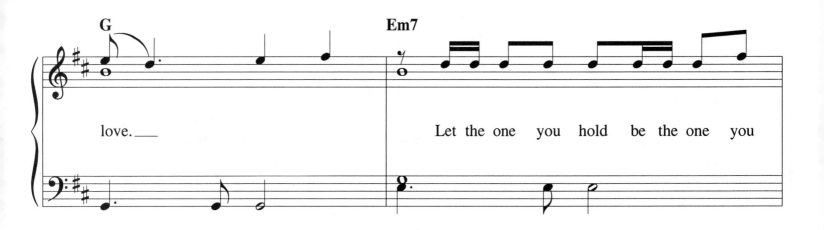

love. ___   Let the one you hold be the one you

want,   the one you need,   'cause when it's all for one it's one for

all. _____ When there's some-one that should know then just

let your feel-ings show and make it all for one and all for

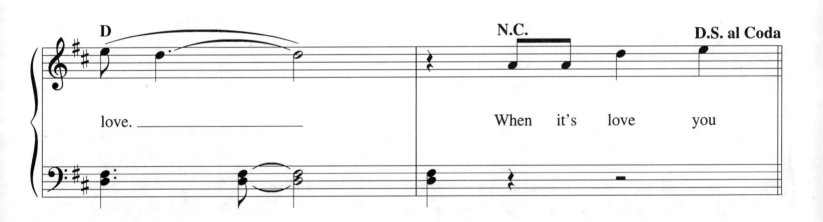

love. _____ When it's love you

love. _____ Don't lay our

love   to rest _ 'cause we could stand up to the test.   We got   ev - 'ry-thing_   and

more   than we   had   planned,   more than the riv-ers   that run _ the land. _

_____ We've got it all _____   in our hands.   Now it's

all   for one and all for   love. _   Let the one you hold be the one you

ALWAYS BE MY BABY

Words and Music by MARIAH CAREY,
JERMAINE DUPRI and MANUEL SEAL

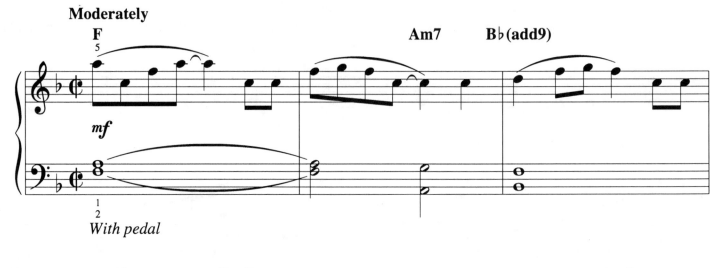

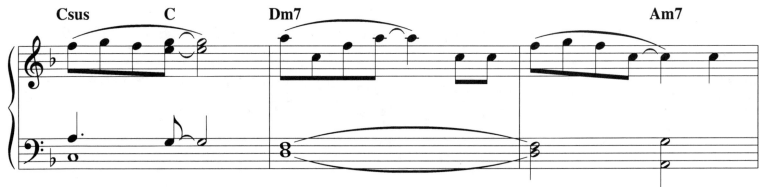

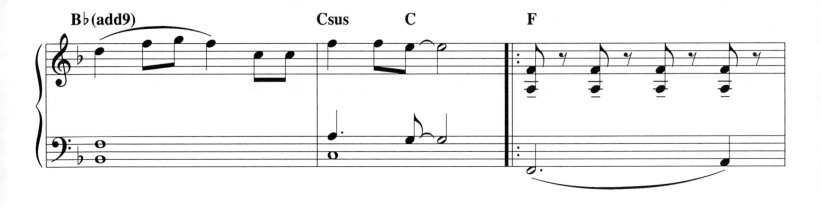

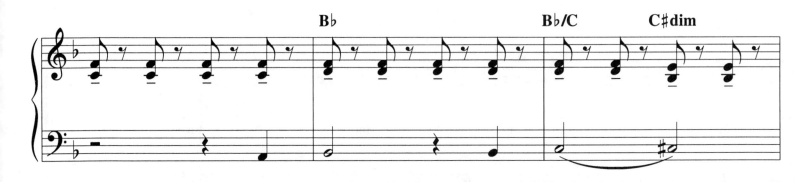

Copyright © 1995 Sony/ATV Songs LLC, Rye Songs, EMI April Music Inc., So So Def Music, Air Control Music and Full Keel Music Co.
All Rights on behalf of Sony/ATV Songs LLC and Rye Songs Administered by Sony/ATV Music Publishing, 8 Music Square West, Nashville, TN 37203
All Rights on behalf of So So Def Music and Air Control Music Controlled and Administered by EMI April Music Inc.
International Copyright Secured   All Rights Reserved

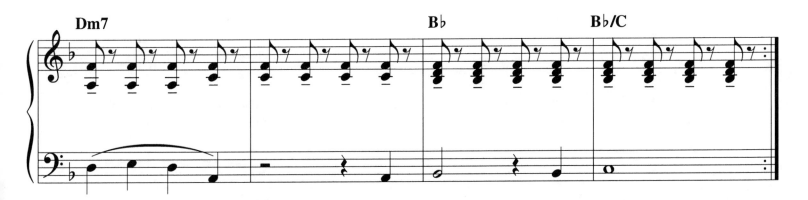

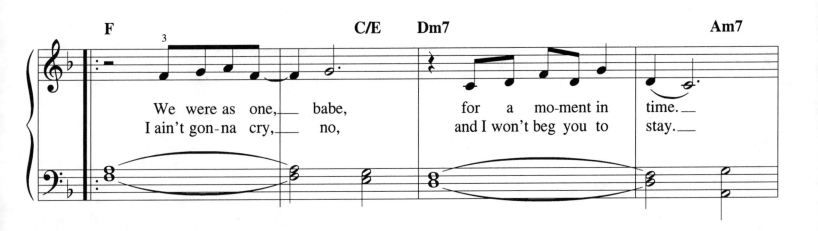

We were as one, ___ babe, for a mo-ment in time. ___
I ain't gon-na cry, ___ no, and I won't beg you to stay. ___

And it seemed ev - er - last - ing, that you would al - ways be
If you're de - ter - mined to leave, ___ boy, I will not stand in your

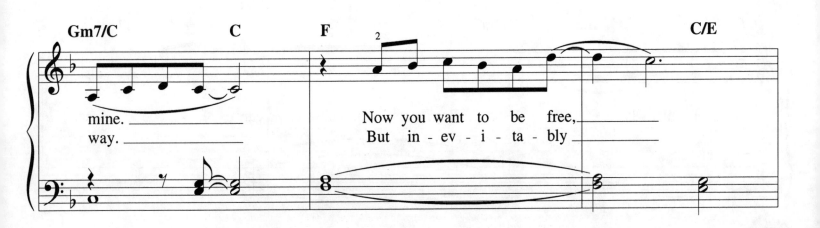

mine. _____ Now you want to be free, ___
way. _____ But in - ev - i - ta - bly ___

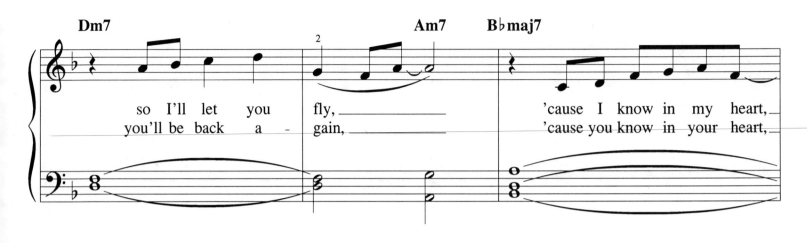

so I'll let you fly, _____ 'cause I know in my heart,
you'll be back a - gain, _____ 'cause you know in your heart,

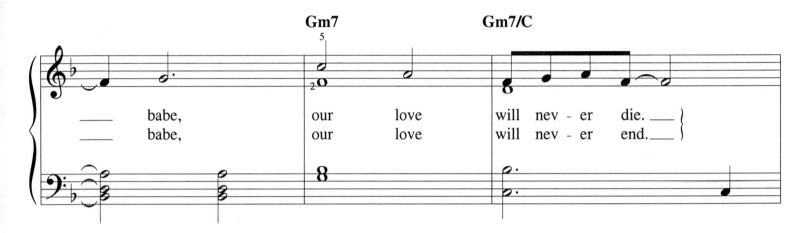

_____ babe, our love will nev - er die. ___ }
_____ babe, our love will nev - er end. ___ }

You'll al - ways be a part of me. ___ I'm part of you in -

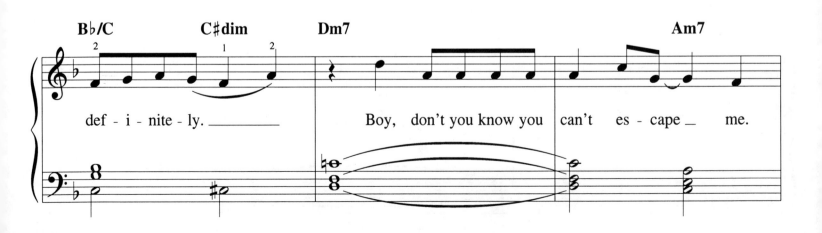

def - i - nite - ly. _____ Boy, don't you know you can't es - cape ___ me.

Ooh dar-ling, 'cause you'll al - ways be ___ my ba - by. And we'll

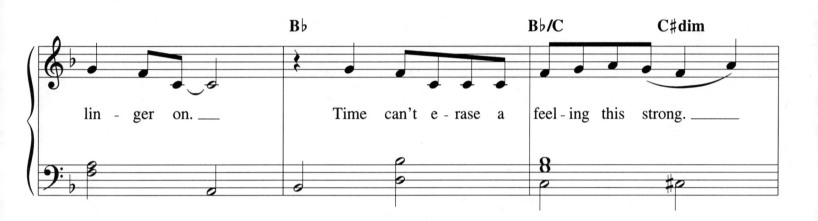

lin - ger on. ___ Time can't e - rase a feel - ing this strong. _____

No way you're ev - er gon - na shake ___ me. Ooh dar - ling, 'cause you'll

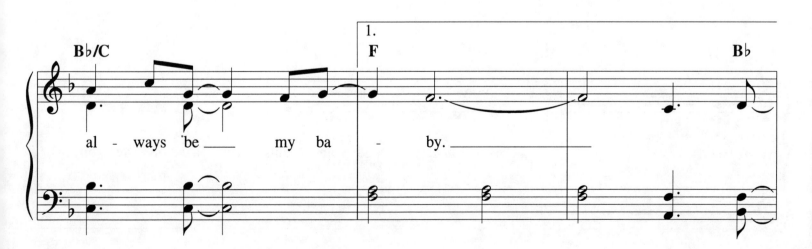

al - ways be ___ my ba - by. _____

- by. I know that you'll be back, boy, when your days and your nights get a lit - tle bit

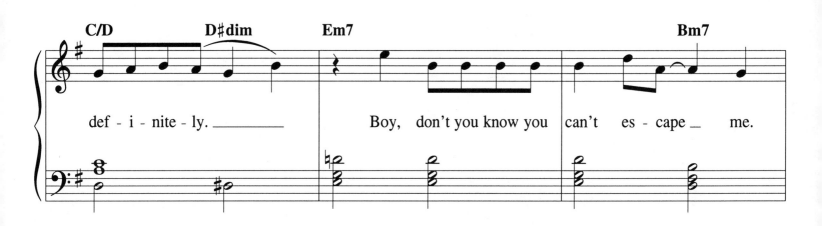

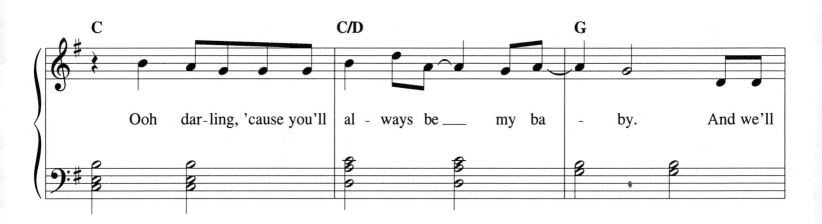

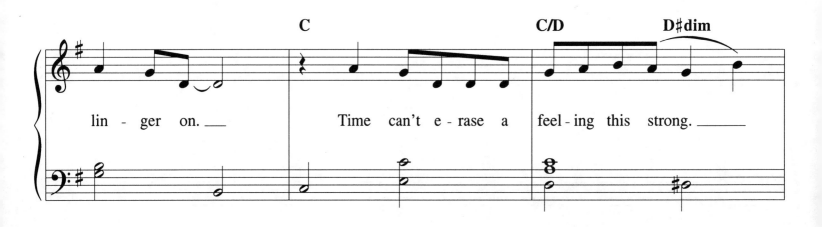

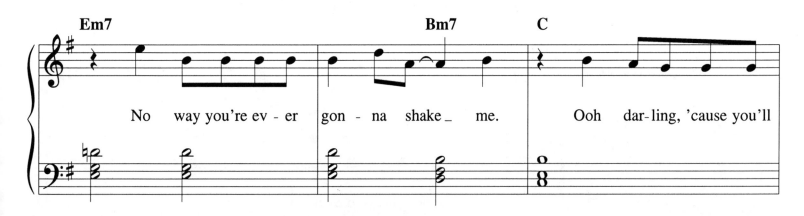

No way you're ev - er gon - na shake_ me. Ooh dar-ling, 'cause you'll

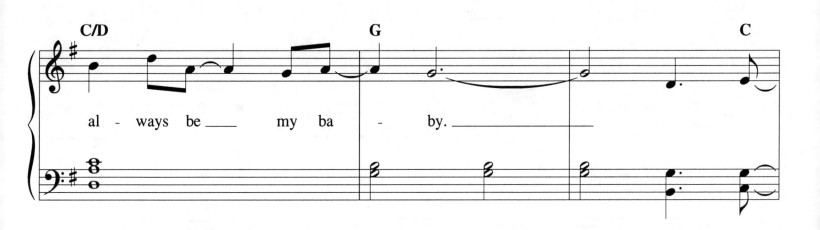

al - ways be ____ my ba - by. ____

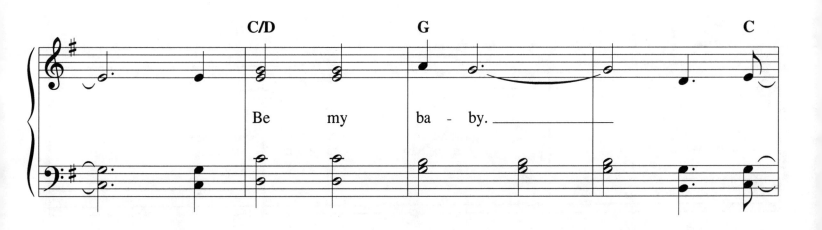

Be my ba - by. _____

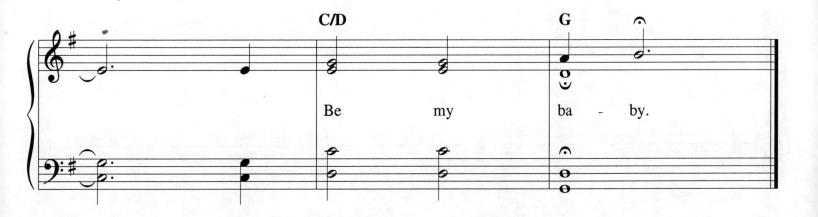

Be my ba - by.

ALWAYS ON MY MIND

Words and Music by WAYNE THOMPSON,
MARK JAMES and JOHNNY CHRISTOPHER

© 1971, 1979 SCREEN GEMS-EMI MUSIC INC. and BUDDE SONGS INC.
All Rights Controlled and Administered by SCREEN GEMS-EMI MUSIC INC.
All Rights Reserved   International Copyright Secured   Used by Permission

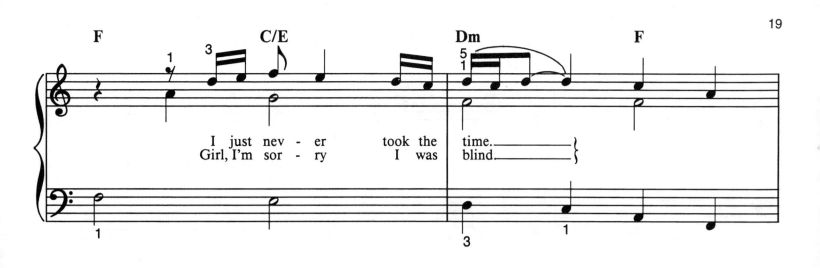

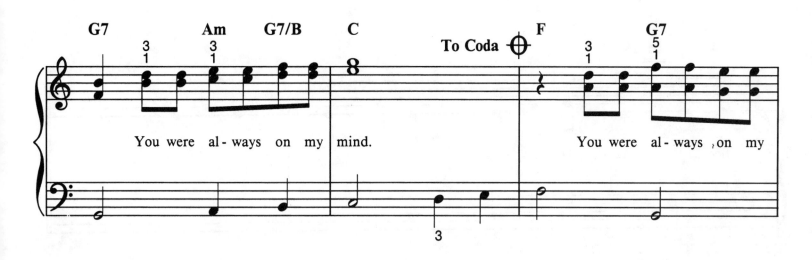

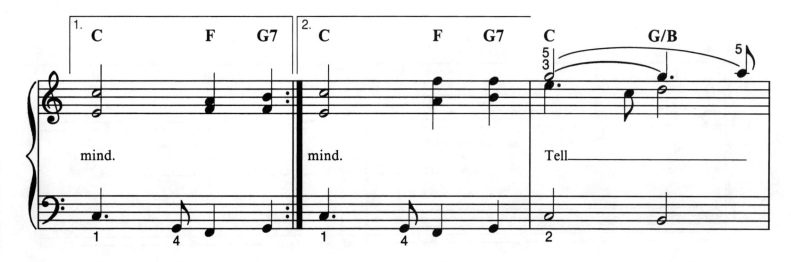

20

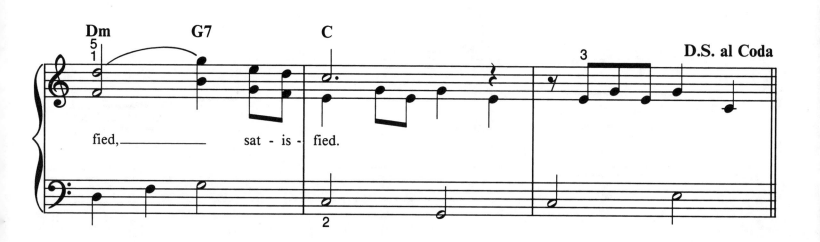

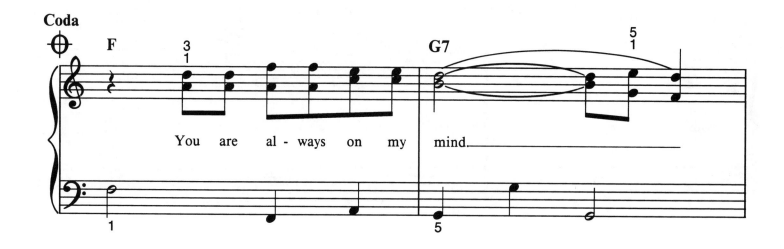

BEAUTY AND THE BEAST
from Walt Disney's BEAUTY AND THE BEAST

Lyrics by HOWARD ASHMAN
Music by ALAN MENKEN

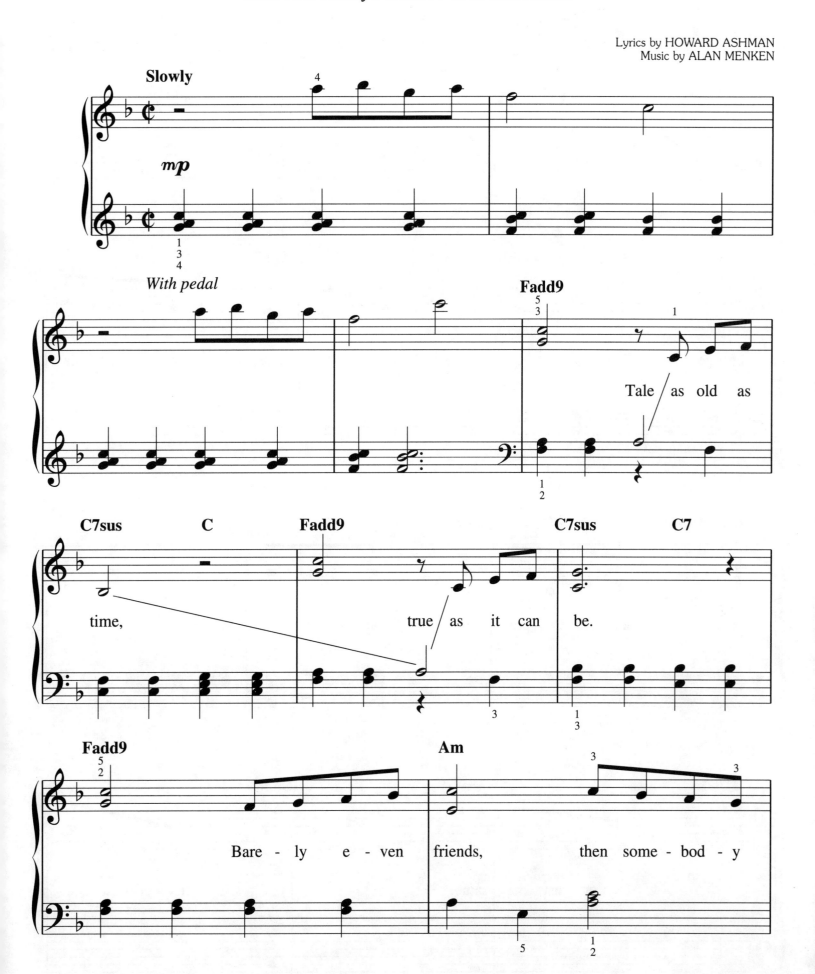

© 1991 Walt Disney Music Company and Wonderland Music Company, Inc.
International Copyright Secured   All Rights Reserved

22

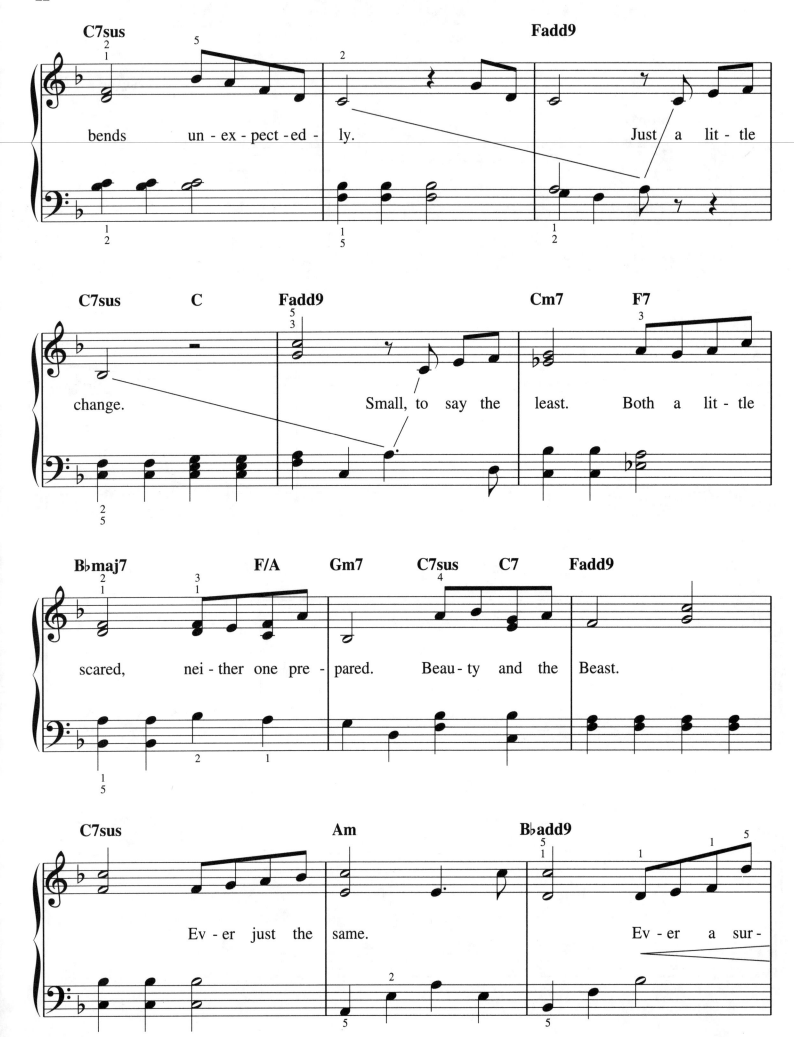

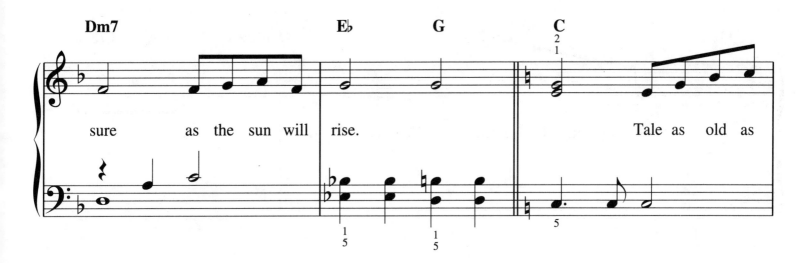

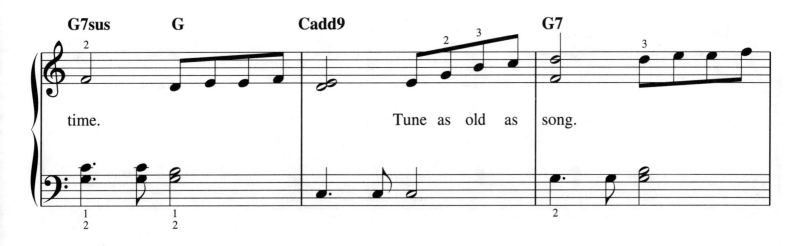

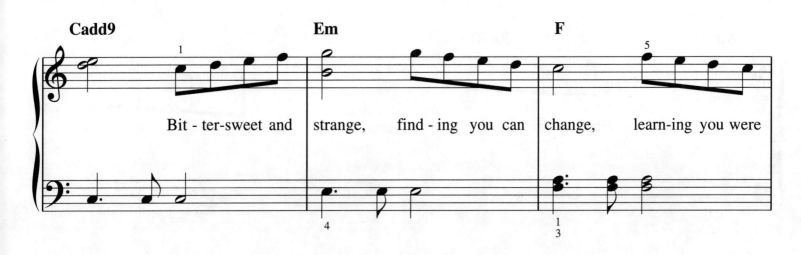

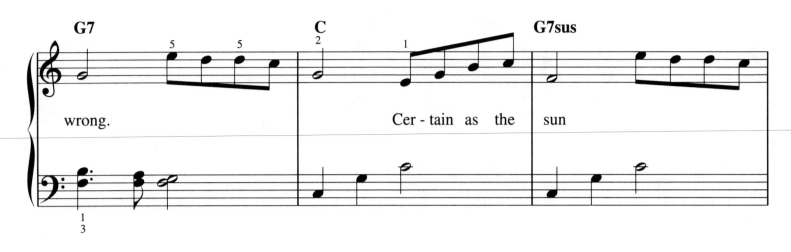

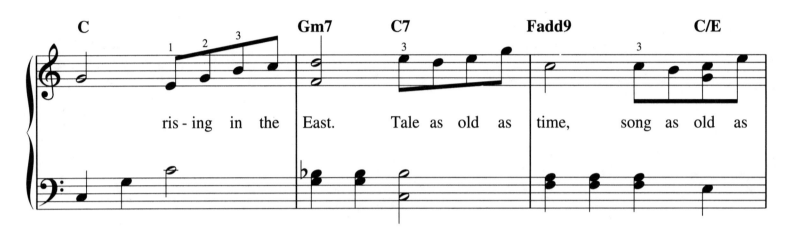

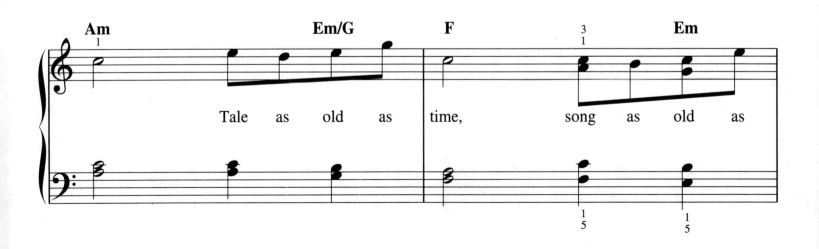

ANYTIME YOU NEED A FRIEND

Words and Music by MARIAH CAREY
and WALTER AFANASIEFF

Copyright © 1993 Sony/ATV Songs LLC, Rye Songs, WB Music Corp. and Wallyworld Music
All Rights on behalf of Sony/ATV Songs LLC and Rye Songs Administered by Sony/ATV Music Publishing, 8 Music Square West, Nashville, TN 37203
All Rights on behalf of Wallyworld Music Administered by WB Music Corp.
International Copyright Secured   All Rights Reserved

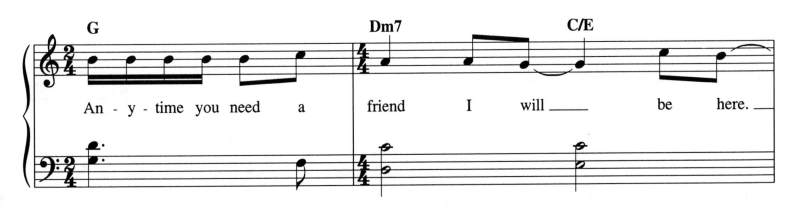

An - y - time you need a friend I will _____ be here. _____

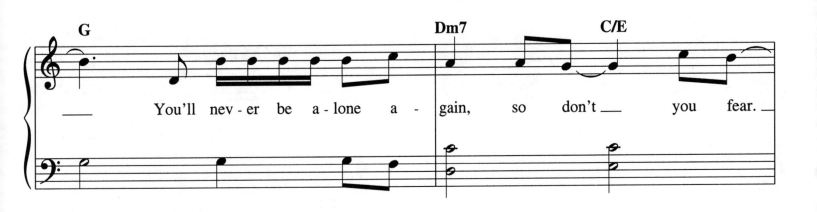

_____ You'll nev - er be a - lone a - gain, so don't _____ you fear. _____

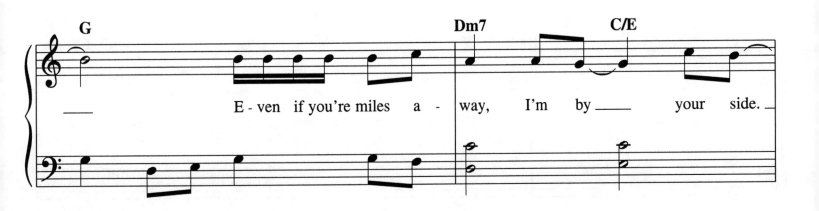

_____ E - ven if you're miles a - way, I'm by _____ your side. _____

_____ So don't you ev - er be lone - ly.

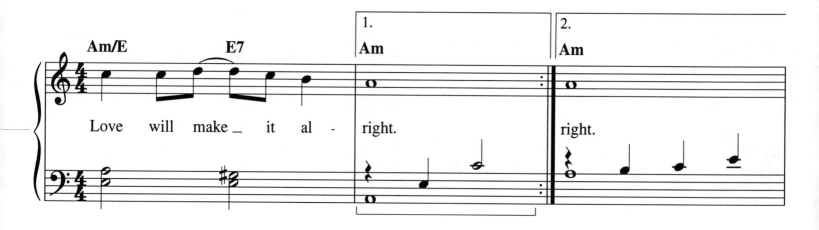

Am/E   E7   1. Am   2. Am

Love will make _ it al - right.   right.   right.

Cdim   G/B   Em7♭5/B♭

If you just be - lieve _ in me   I will love you end -

F/A   Dm7♭5/A♭   C/G   F♯m7♭5

- less - ly.   Take my hand. Take me   in - to your heart. _

Fmaj7   F6   Esus   E   G

I'll be there for - ev - er, ba - by.   I won't let go. _ I'll nev - er let   go. _ An - y - time you need a

BEAUTIFUL IN MY EYES

Words and Music by
JOSHUA KADISON

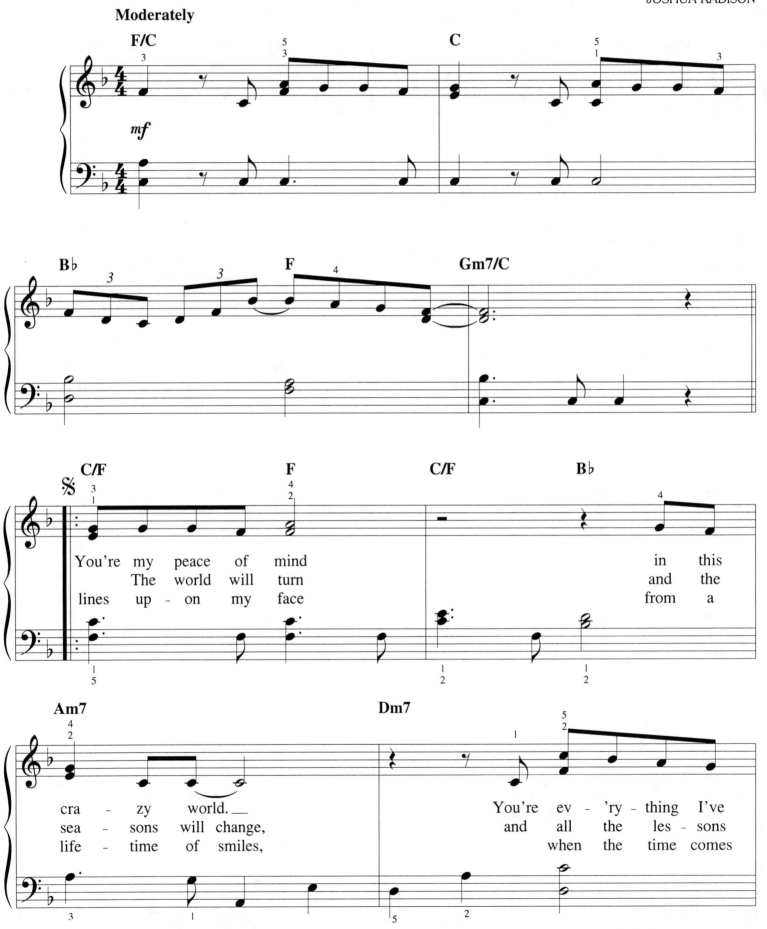

© 1993 JOSHUASONGS, EMI BLACKWOOD MUSIC INC. and SEYMOUR GLASS MUSIC
All Rights Controlled and Administered by EMI BLACKWOOD MUSIC INC.
All Rights Reserved   International Copyright Secured   Used by Permission

you'll al - ways be beau - ti - ful in my

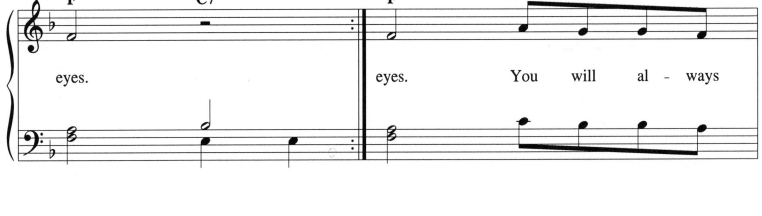

1.

eyes.

2.,3.

eyes. You will al - ways

be beau - ti - ful in my eyes. _____

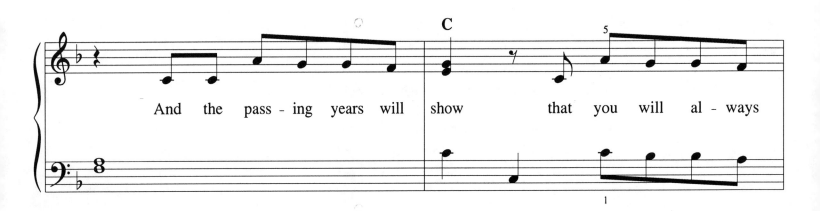

And the pass - ing years will show that you will al - ways

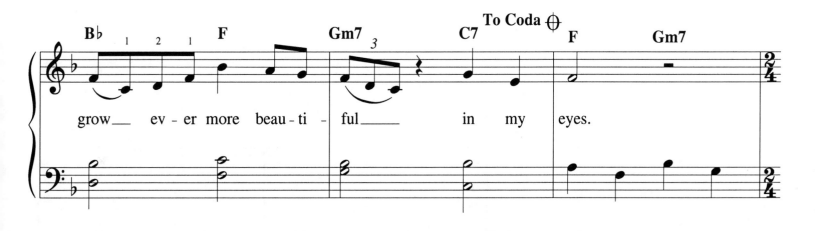

grow___ ev - er more beau-ti - ful_____ in my eyes.

When there are

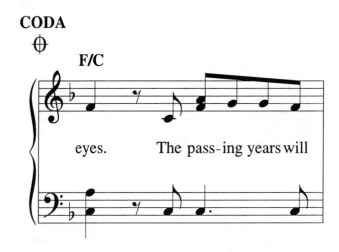

eyes. The pass-ing years will

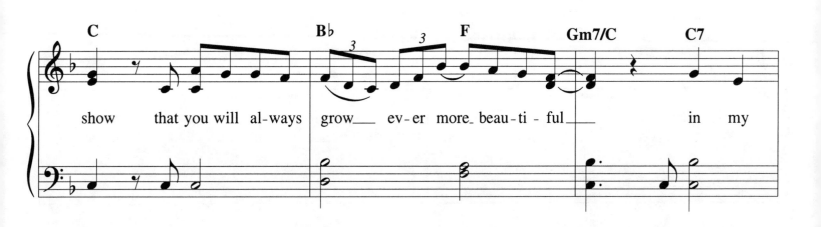

show that you will al-ways grow___ ev-er more_ beau-ti - ful_____ in my

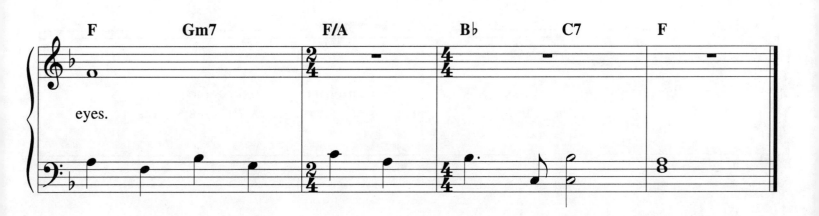

eyes.

CAN YOU FEEL THE LOVE TONIGHT
from Walt Disney Pictures' THE LION KING

Music by ELTON JOHN
Lyrics by TIM RICE

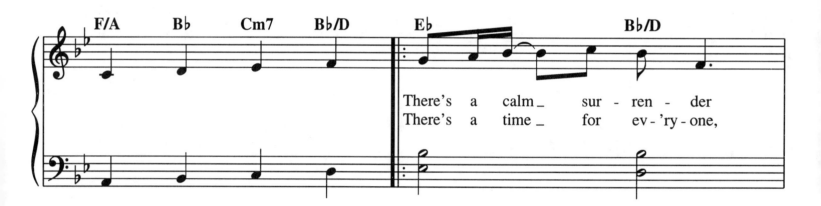

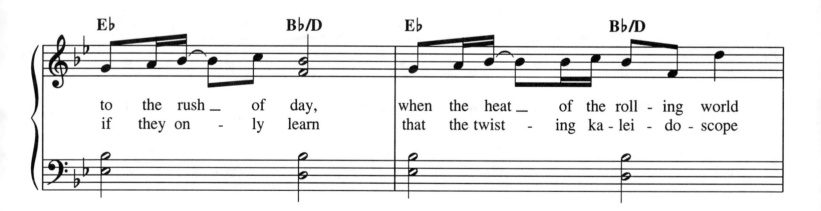

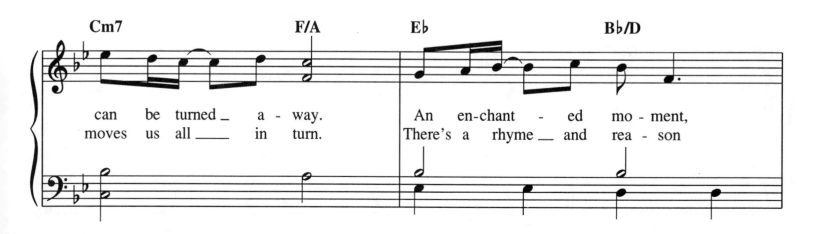

© 1994 Wonderland Music Company, Inc.
International Copyright Secured   All Rights Reserved

wide - eyed wan-der-er _____ that we got this far. ___

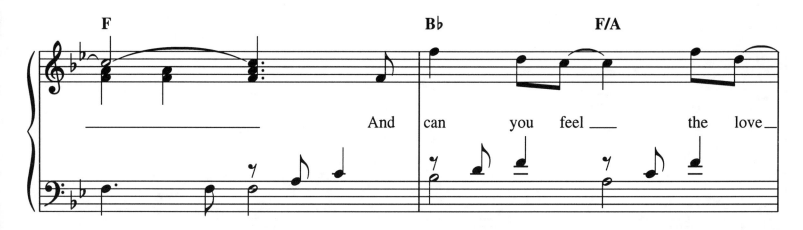

_____ And can you feel ___ the love ___

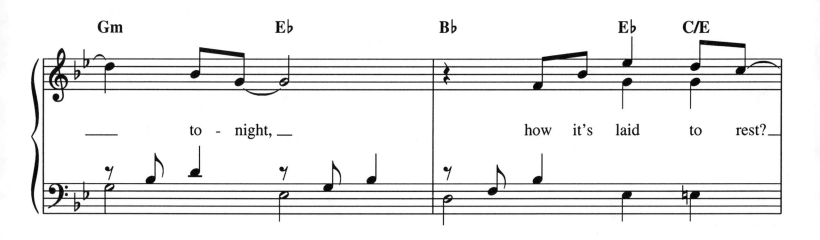

___ to - night, ___ how it's laid to rest?

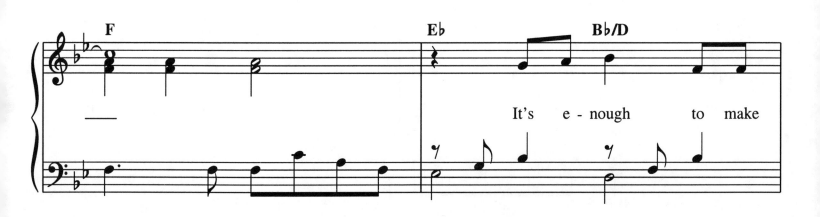

___ It's e-nough to make

CHANGE THE WORLD
featured on the Motion Picture Soundtrack PHENOMENON

Words and Music by GORDON KENNEDY,
TOMMY SIMS and WAYNE KIRKPATRICK

Copyright © 1996 PolyGram International Publishing, Inc., Careers-BMG Music Publishing, Inc.,
MCA Music Publishing, A Division of Universal Studios, Inc., Bases Loaded Music and Sierra Skye Songs
Bases Loaded Music partially admin. by EMI Christian Music Publishing
International Copyright Secured   All Rights Reserved

...

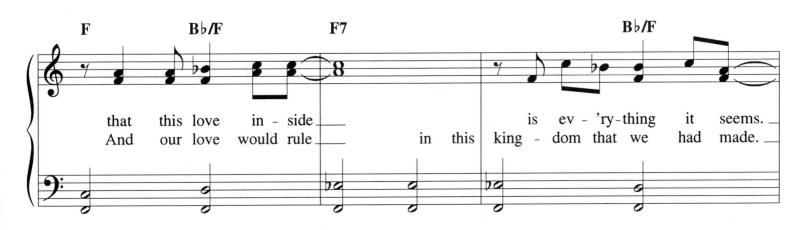

that   this   love   in - side _____   is   ev - 'ry-thing   it   seems. ___
And   our   love   would rule _____   in   this   king - dom that   we   had   made. ___

_____   But   for now   I   find _____
_____   Till then I'll be   a   fool, _____

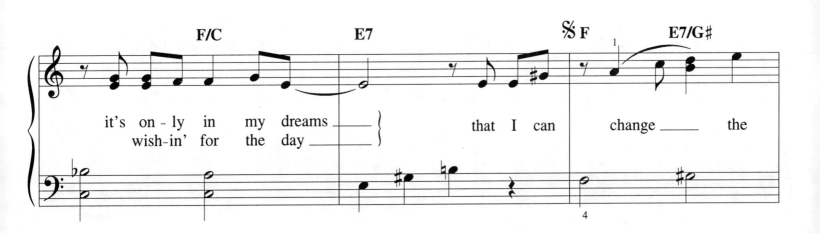

it's   on - ly   in   my   dreams _____   that   I   can   change _____   the
wish-in'   for   the   day _____

world. _____   I would be   the sun-light in your   un - i - verse.

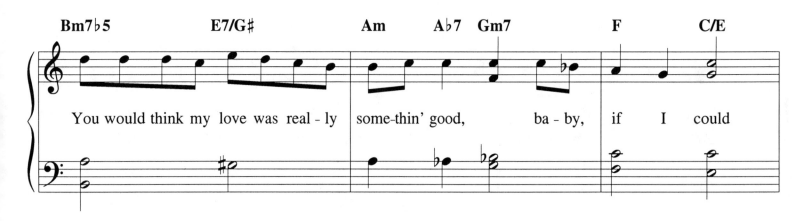

You would think my love was real - ly some-thin' good, ba - by, if I could

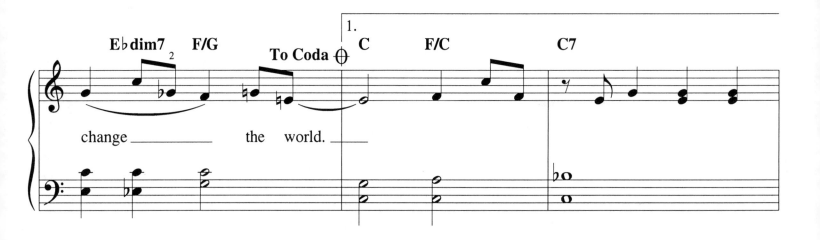

change _____ the world. _____

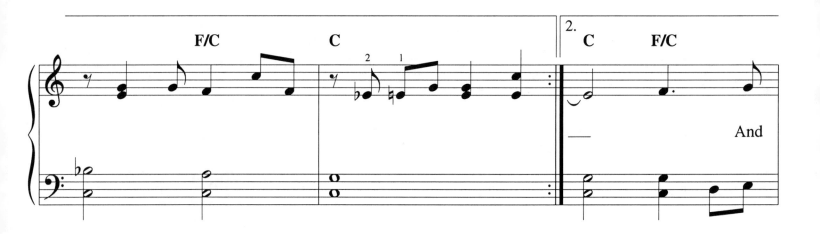

And

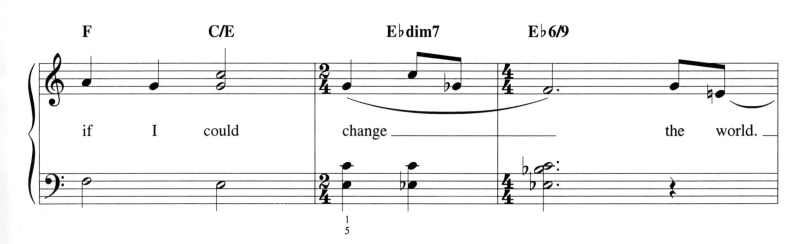

if I could change _____ the world. _____

COULD I HAVE THIS DANCE

from URBAN COWBOY

Words and Music by WAYLAND HOLYFIELD
and BOB HOUSE

Medium Waltz

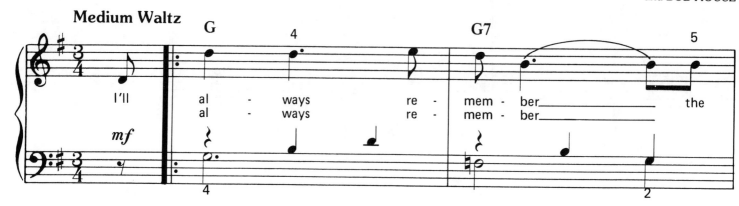

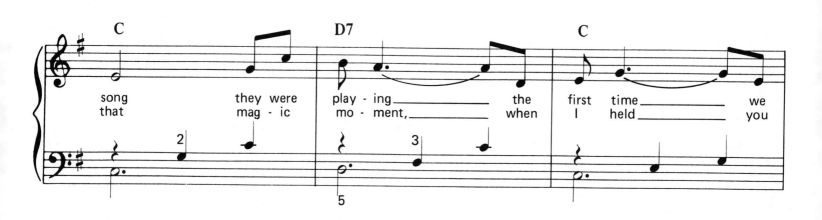

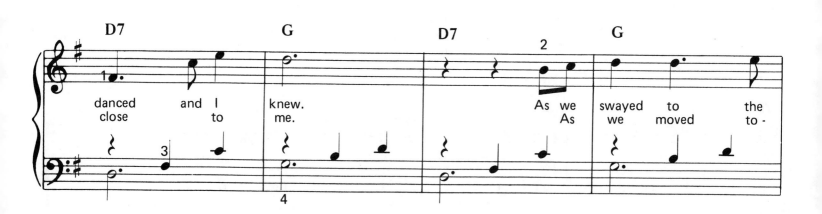

Copyright © 1980 Sony/ATV Songs LLC and PolyGram International Publishing, Inc.
All Rights on behalf of Sony/ATV Songs LLC Administered by Sony/ATV Music Publishing, 8 Music Square West, Nashville, TN 37203
International Copyright Secured   All Rights Reserved

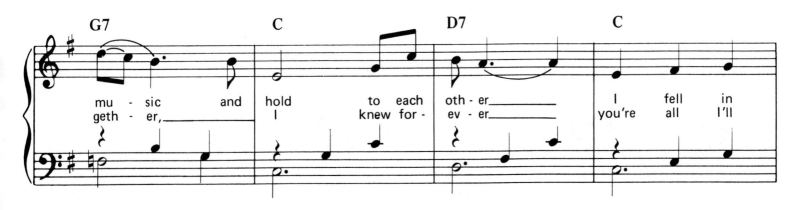

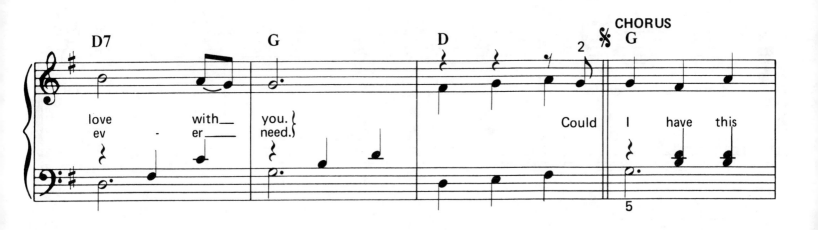

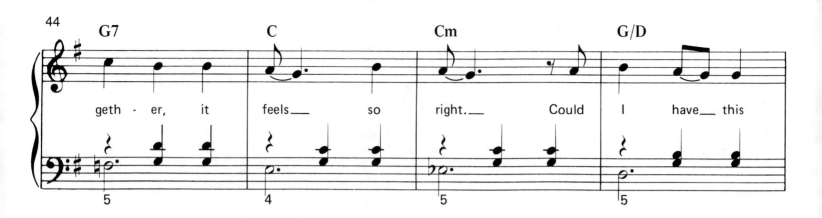

geth - er, it feels___ so right.___ Could I have___ this

dance for the rest of my___ life? I'll

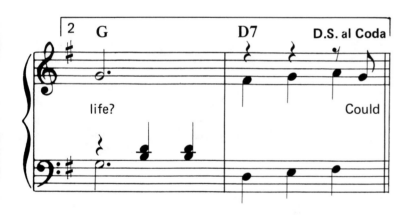

life? Could

rest of my___

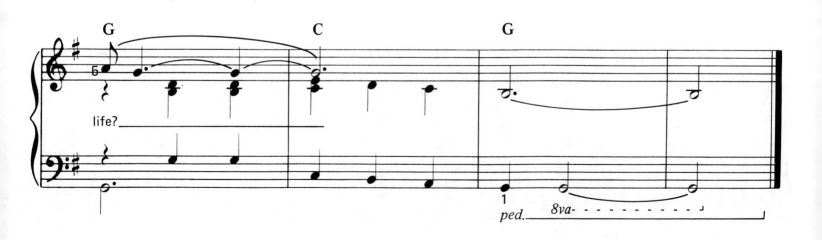

life?___

ped. *8va- - - - - - - - - - - -*

DON'T KNOW MUCH

Words and Music by BARRY MANN,
CYNTHIA WEIL and TOM SNOW

© 1980 SONY/ATV SONGS LLC, MANN & WEIL SONGS, INC., EMI BLACKWOOD MUSIC INC. and SNOW MUSIC
All Rights for SONY/ATV SONGS LLC and MANN & WEIL SONGS, INC. Controlled and Administered by EMI BLACKWOOD MUSIC INC.
All Rights Reserved   International Copyright Secured   Used by Permission

I don't know much, but I know I love you, _____ and that may be _____ all I need to

ENDLESS LOVE

Words and Music by
LIONEL RICHIE

Copyright © 1981 by PGP Music and Brockman Music
All Rights Administered by Intersong U.S.A., Inc.
International Copyright Secured   All Rights Reserved

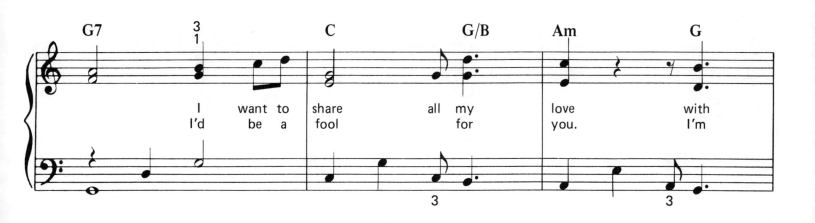

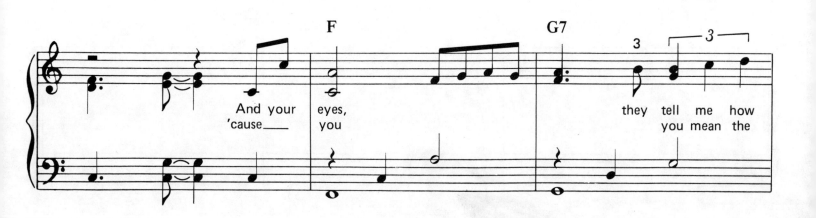

much | you | care. | Oh___ yes, | you will
world | to | me. | Oh___ I know | I___

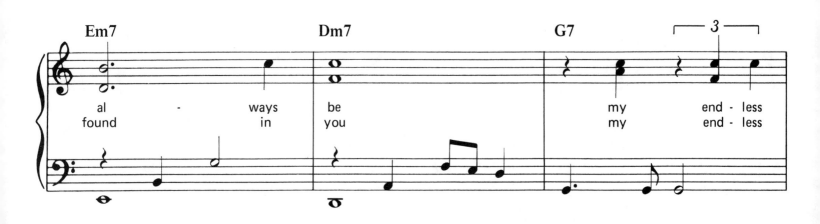

al - ways | be | my end - less
found in | you | my end - less

love. | *dim.* | love.

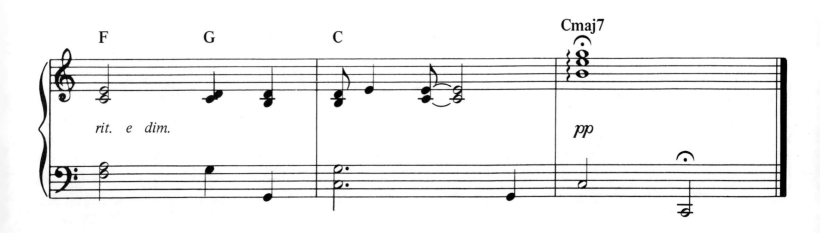

rit. e dim. | *pp*

FIELDS OF GOLD

Words and Music by
STING

Flowing, moderately

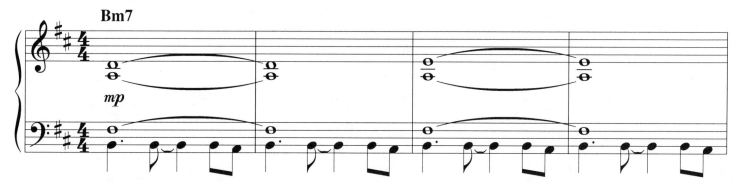

mem-ber me ___ when the west wind moves __ up - on the fields __ of
stay with me, __ will you be my love __ a - mong the fields __ of

bar - ley. You'll for - get the sun __ in his jeal - ous sky __ as we
bar - ley? We'll for - get the sun __ in his jeal - ous sky __ as we

Copyright © 1992 Gordon M. Sumner Represented by Magnetic Publishing Ltd. (PRS)
Represented by Reggatta Music Ltd. (BMI) and Administered by Irving Music, Inc. (BMI) in the U.S. and Canada
International Copyright Secured   All Rights Reserved

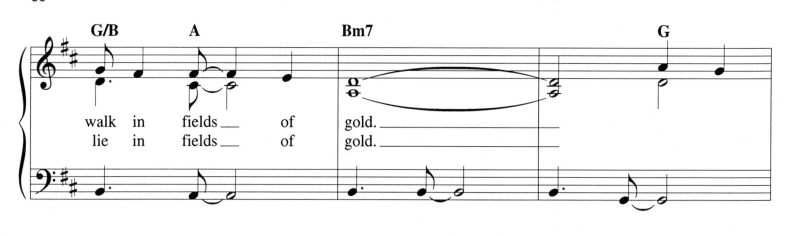

walk in fields ___ of gold. _____
lie in fields ___ of gold. _____

So she took her love ___ for to
See the west wind move ___ like a

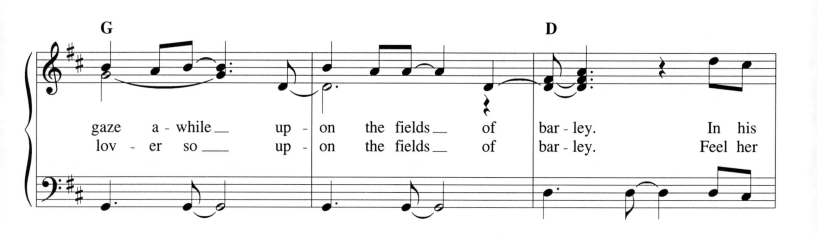

gaze a-while ___ up - on the fields ___ of bar - ley. In his
lov - er so ___ up - on the fields ___ of bar - ley. Feel her

arms she fell ___ as her hair came down ___ a - mong the fields ___ of
bod - y rise ___ when you kiss her mouth ___ a - mong the fields ___ of

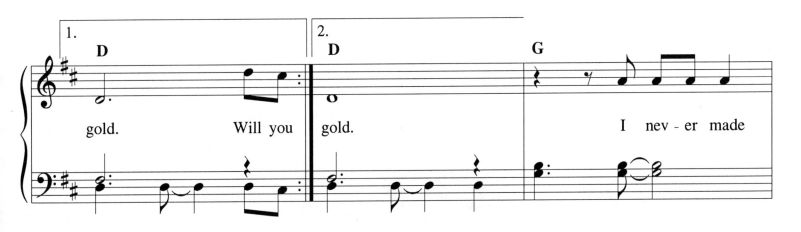

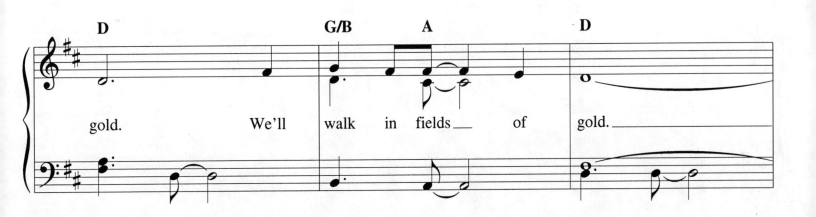

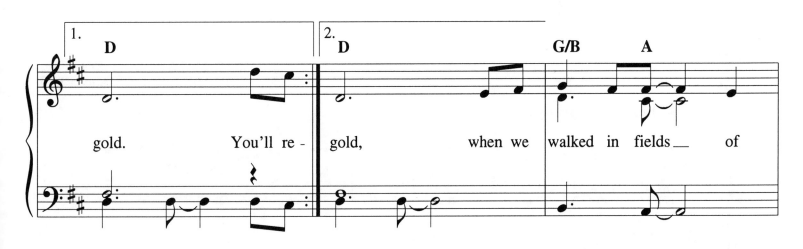

gold.   You'll re -   gold,   when we   walked in fields ___   of

gold,   when we   walked   in   fields ___   of

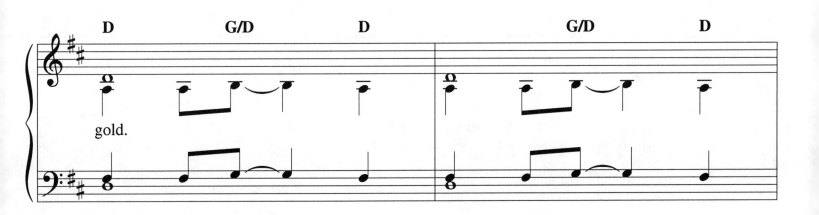

gold.

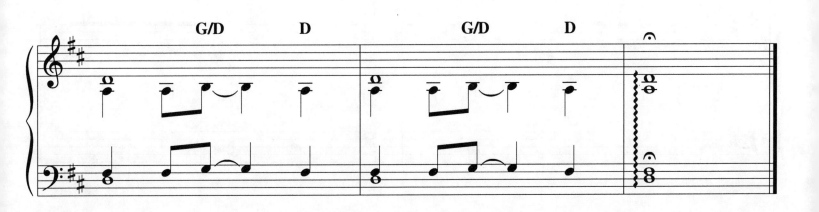

ETERNAL FLAME

Words and Music by BILLY STEINBERG,
TOM KELLY and SUSANNA HOFFS

Copyright © 1988 Sony/ATV Tunes LLC, EMI Blackwood Music Inc. and Bangophile Music
All Rights on behalf of Sony/ATV Tunes LLC Administered by Sony/ATV Music Publishing, 8 Music Square West, Nashville, TN 37203
All Rights on behalf of Bangophile Music Controlled and Administered by EMI Blackwood Music Inc.
International Copyright Secured   All Rights Reserved

FOREVER IN LOVE

By KENNY G

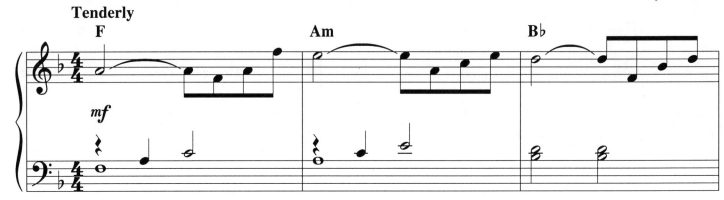

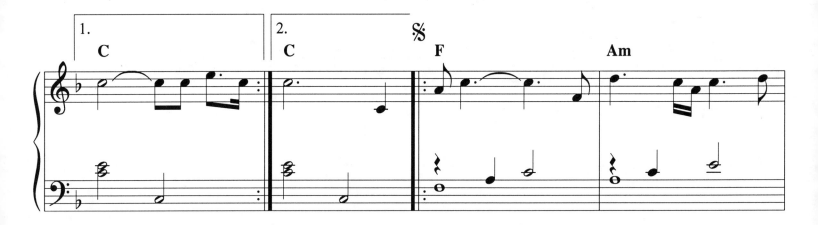

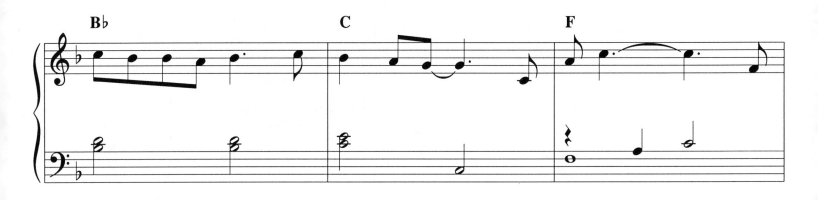

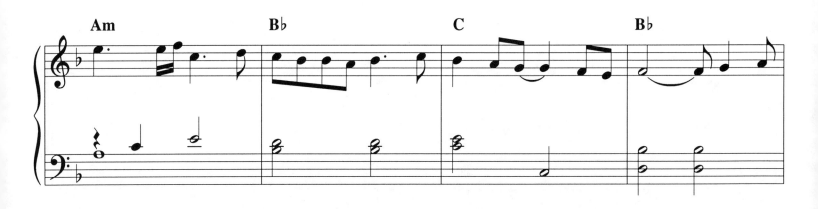

© 1992 EMI BLACKWOOD MUSIC INC., KUZU MUSIC, KENNY G MUSIC and HIGH TECH MUSIC
All Rights for KUZU MUSIC Controlled and Administered by EMI BLACKWOOD MUSIC INC.
All Rights Reserved   International Copyright Secured   Used by Permission

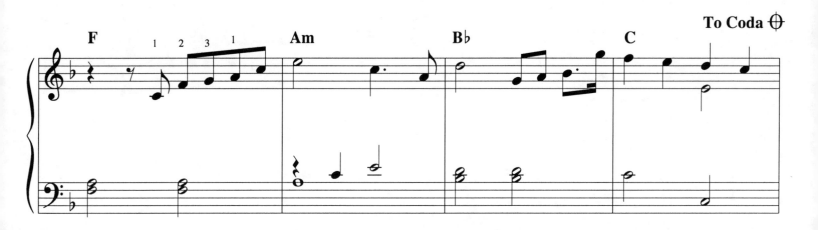

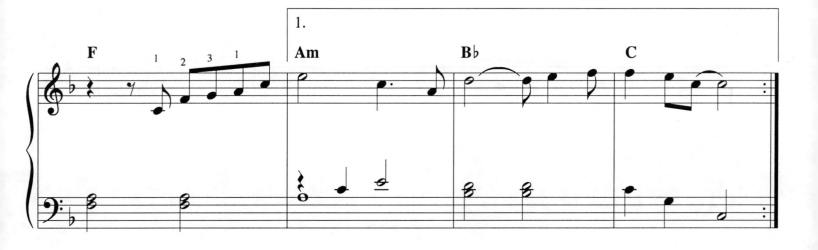

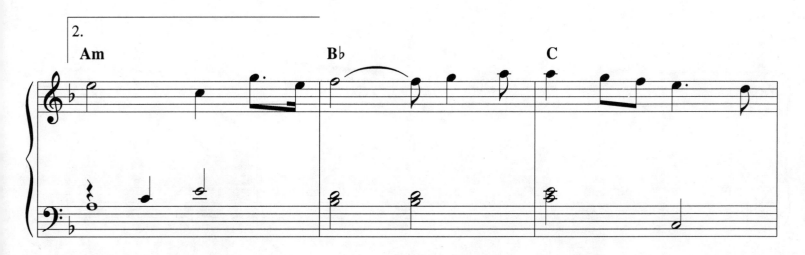

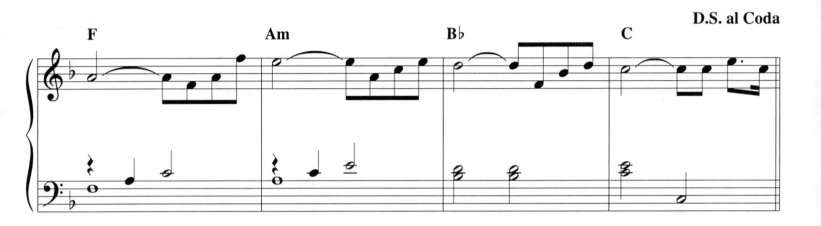

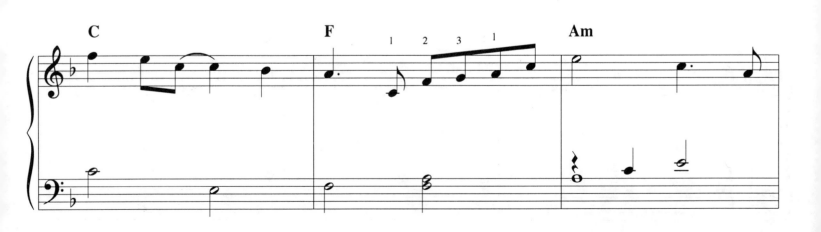

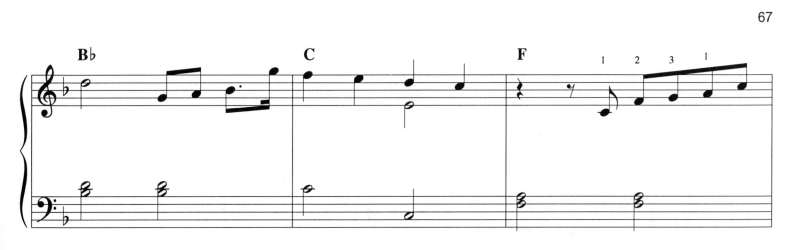

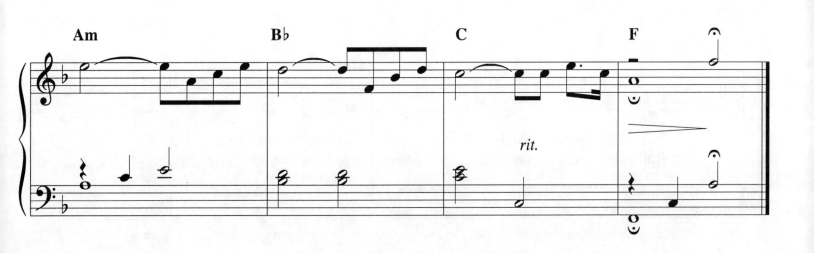

GOOD FOR ME

Words and Music by JAY GRUSKA, AMY GRANT,
TOM SNOW and WAYNE KIRKPATRICK

With a steady beat

You like to dance ___ and
You like to drive ___ like

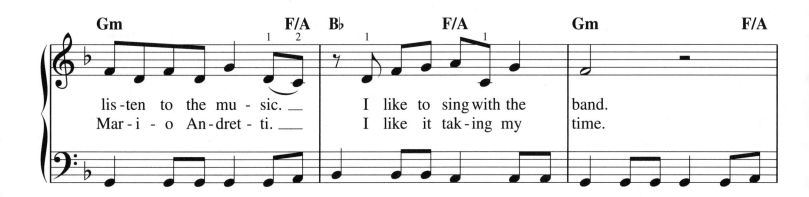

lis-ten to the mu-sic. ___ I like to sing with the band.
Mar-i-o An-dret-ti. ___ I like it tak-ing my time.

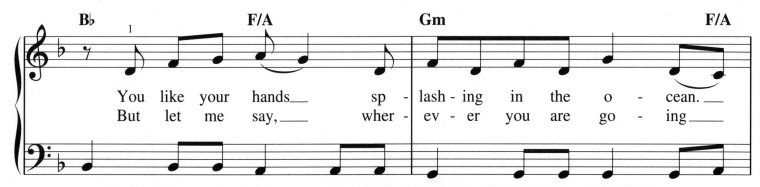

You like your hands ___ spl-ash-ing in the o - cean. ___
But let me say, ___ wher - ev-er you are go - ing ___

© Copyright 1991 by J-88 MUSIC, MCA - GEFFEN MUSIC, AGE TO AGE MUSIC, INC., CAREERS-BMG MUSIC PUBLISHING, INC. and TOM SNOW MUSIC
All Rights for J-88 MUSIC Controlled and Administered by MCA - GEFFEN MUSIC
All Rights for AGE TO AGE MUSIC, INC. Administered by BH PUBLISHING
International Copyright Secured   All Rights Reserved

MCA music publishing

I like my feet on the sand.
you know it suits me just fine.

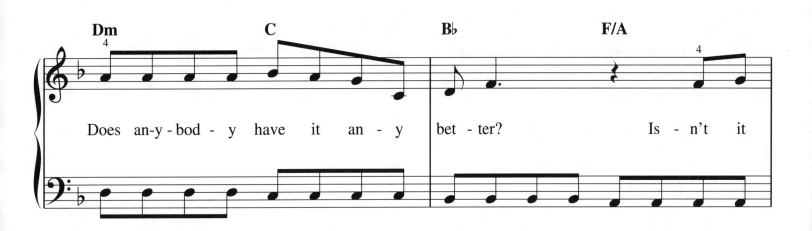

Does an-y-bod - y have it an - y bet - ter? Is - n't it

eas - y to see just how well we fit to - geth - er?

When I start to sing the blues you pull out my danc-ing shoes. I think

you could be so good for me.

You get brave when I get shy. Just an - oth - er rea - son why I think

you could be so good for me.

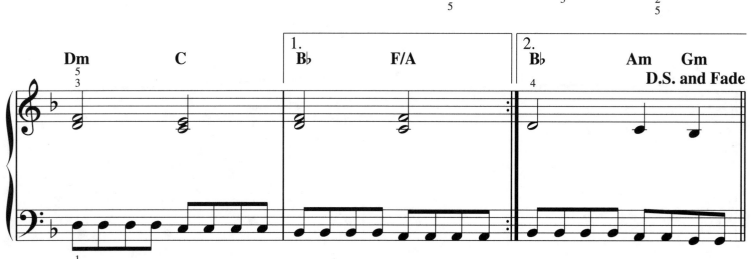

GROW OLD WITH ME

Words and Music by
JOHN LENNON

Copyright © 1982 Ono Music
All Rights Administered by Sony/ATV Music Publishing, 8 Music Square West, Nashville, TN 37203
International Copyright Secured   All Rights Reserved

HAVE I TOLD YOU LATELY

Words and Music by
VAN MORRISON

Have I told you late-ly that I love you?_____ Have I told you there's no one else a-bove you?_____ Fill my heart with glad-ness, take a-way all my sad-ness, ease my trou-bles that's what you

Copyright © 1989 Caledonia Publishing Ltd.
All Rights for the United States and Canada Administered by Songs Of PolyGram International, Inc.
International Copyright Secured   All Rights Reserved

HERE AND NOW

Words and Music by TERRY STEELE
and DAVID ELLIOT

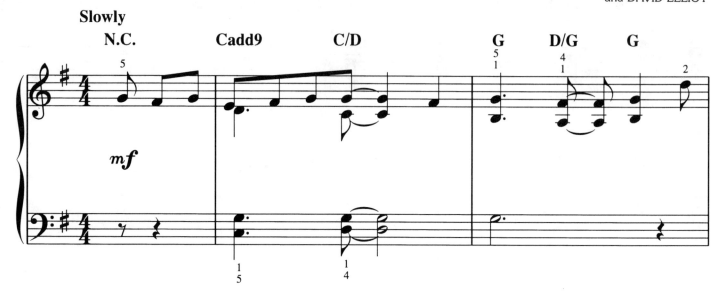

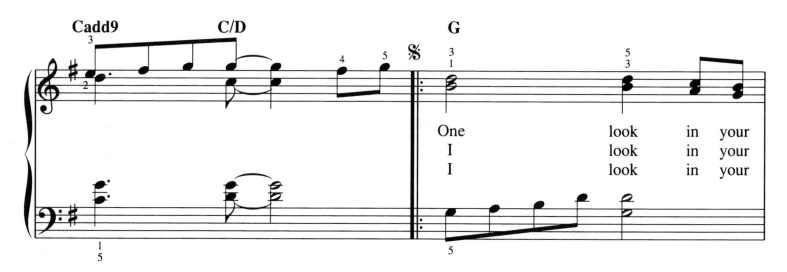

One _____ look in your
I _____ look in your
I _____ look in your

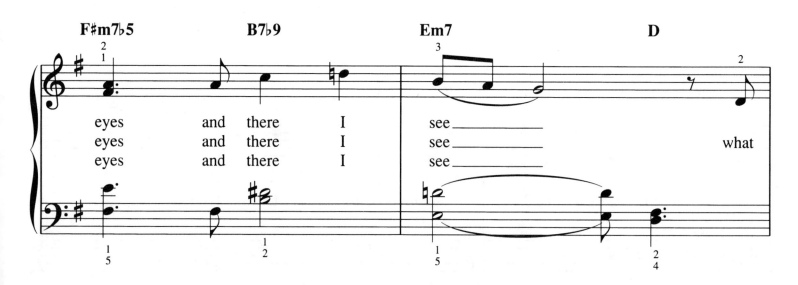

eyes and there I see _____
eyes and there I see _____
eyes and there I see _____ what

© 1989 EMI APRIL MUSIC INC., OLLIE BROWN SUGAR MUSIC and DLE MUSIC
All Rights for OLLIE BROWN SUGAR MUSIC Controlled and Administered by EMI APRIL MUSIC INC.
All Rights Reserved   International Copyright Secured   Used by Permission

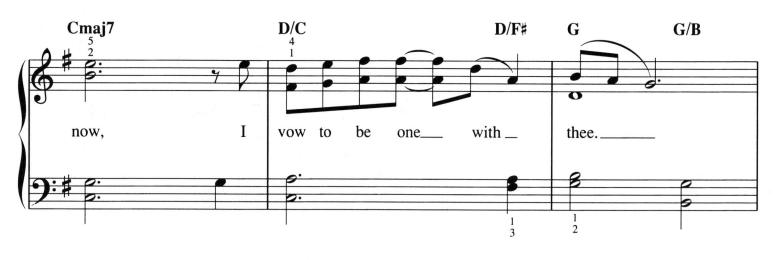

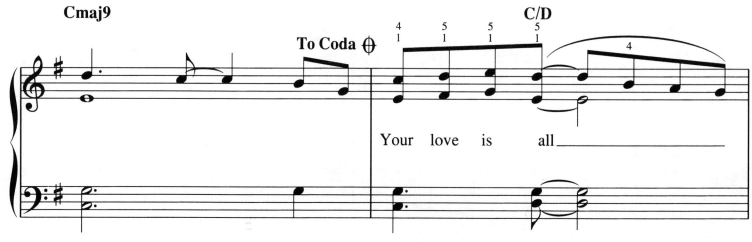

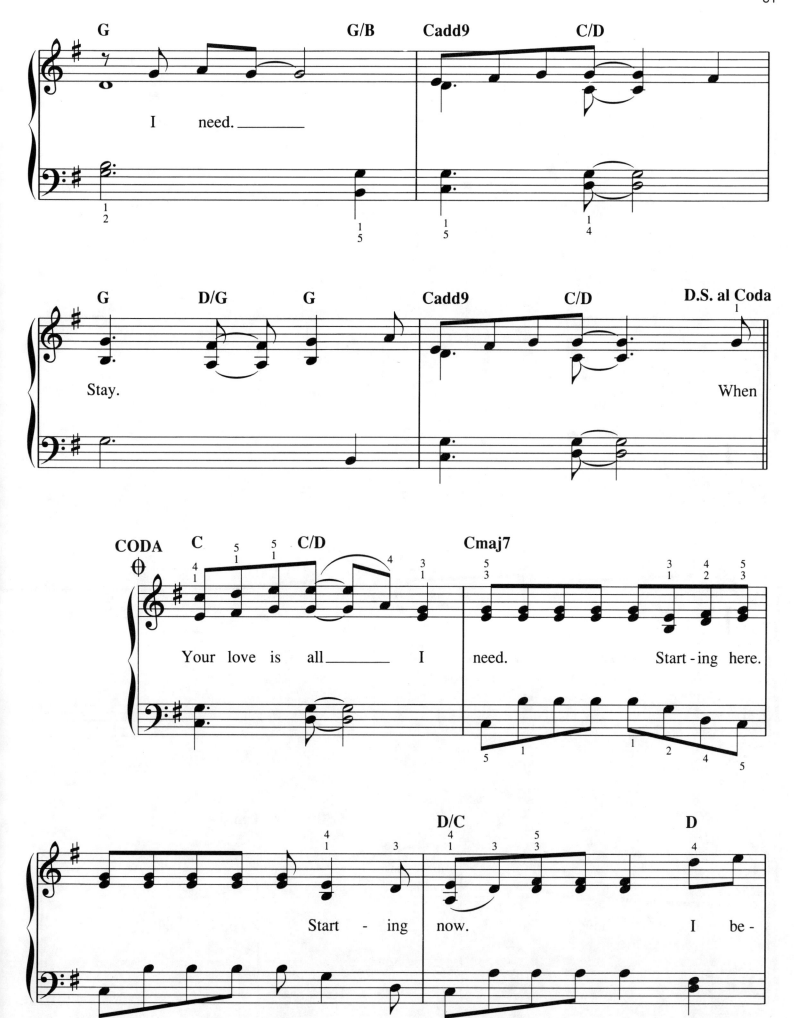

HOW AM I SUPPOSED TO LIVE WITHOUT YOU

Words and Music by MICHAEL BOLTON
and DOUG JAMES

I could hard-ly be-lieve it when I heard the news to-day. I
I'm too proud for cry-ing, did-n't come here to break down. It's just a

had to come and get it straight from you. _____
dream of mine is com-in' to an end. _____

© 1983 EMI APRIL MUSIC INC., IS HOT MUSIC and EMI BLACKWOOD MUSIC INC.
All Rights for IS HOT MUSIC Controlled and Administered by EMI APRIL MUSIC INC.
All Rights Reserved   International Copyright Secured   Used by Permission

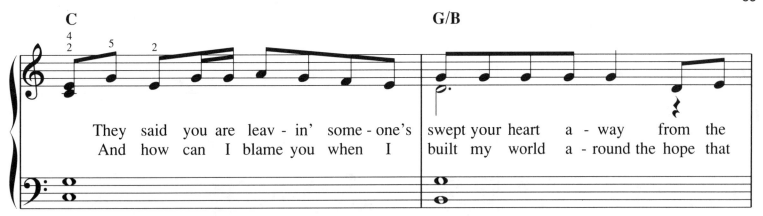

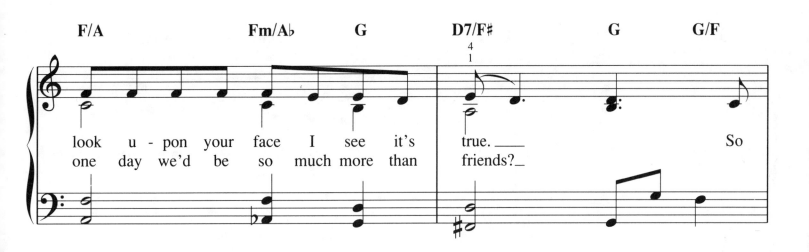

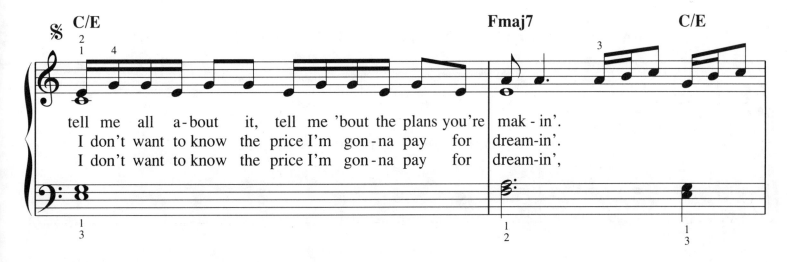

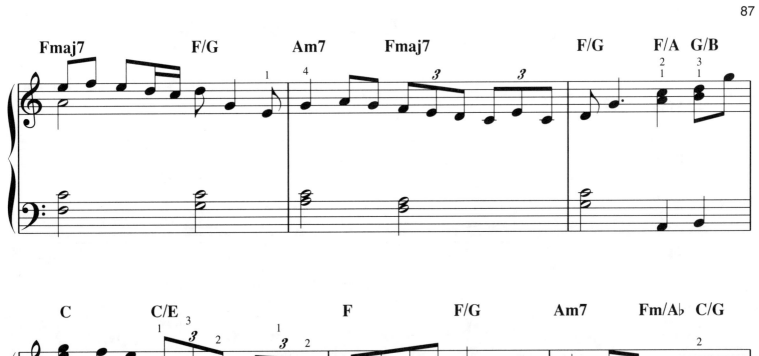

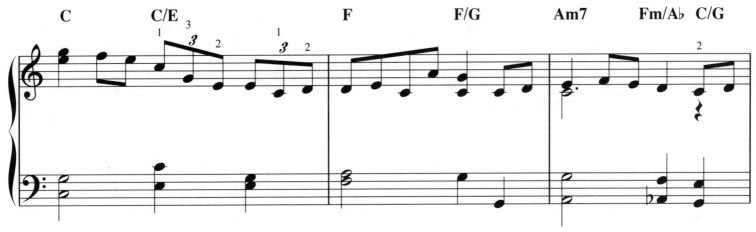

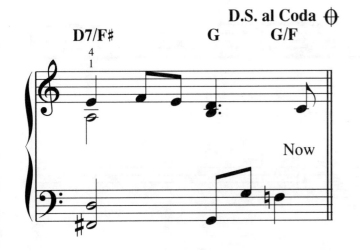

Now

all that I've been liv - ing for is

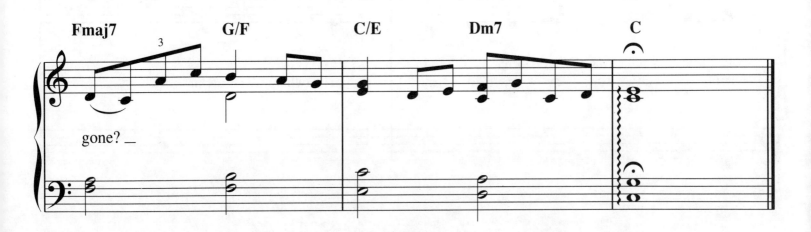

gone? __

I CAN LOVE YOU LIKE THAT

Words and Music by STEVE DIAMOND,
MARIBETH DERRY and JENNIFER KIMBALL

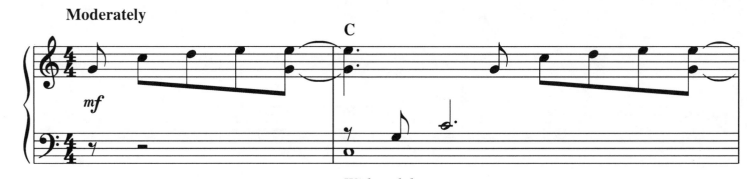

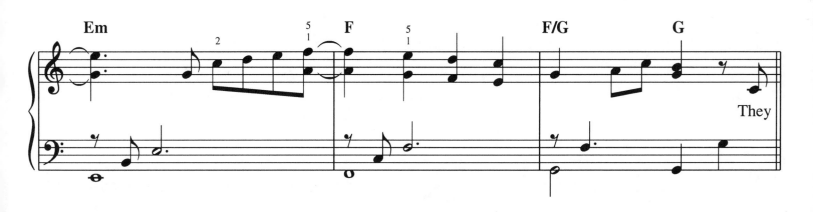

They

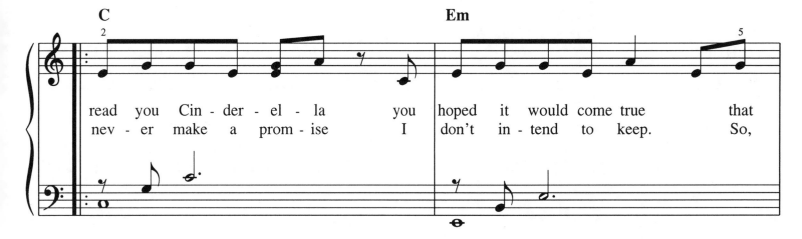

read you Cin-der-el - la   you hoped it would come true   that
nev - er make a prom - ise   I   don't in-tend to keep.   So,

one day your Prince Charm - ing would come ___ res - cue you. ___   You
when I say for - ev - er, for - ev - er's what I mean.

© 1995 Diamond Cuts, Criterion Music Corp., Full Keel Music Co., Second Wave Music and Friends And Angels Music
All Rights for Diamond Cuts in the U.S. and Canada Administered by Seven Summits Music
All Rights for Second Wave Music and Friends And Angels Music Administered by Full Keel Music Co.
International Copyright Secured   All Rights Reserved

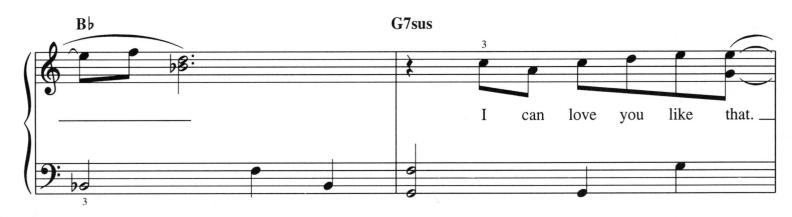

92

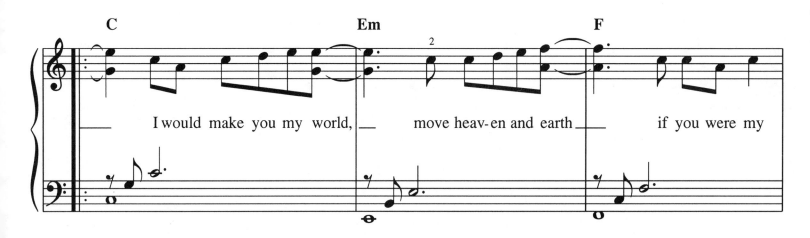

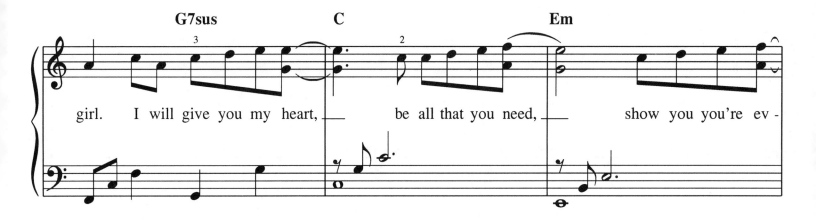

I'LL STILL BE LOVING YOU

Words and Music by TODD CERNEY, PAM ROSE,
MARYANN KENNEDY and PAT BUNCH

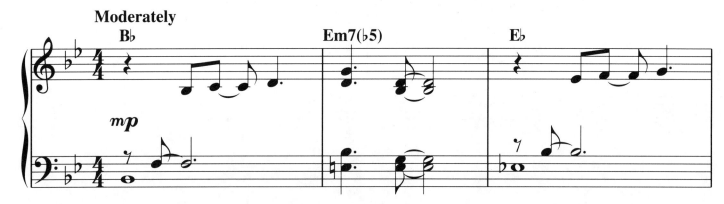

Chang-ing my life with your
Nev-er be - fore did I

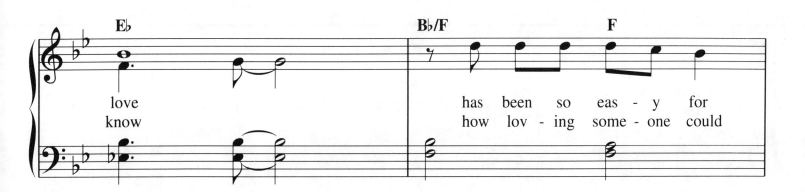

love has been so eas-y for
know how lov-ing some-one could

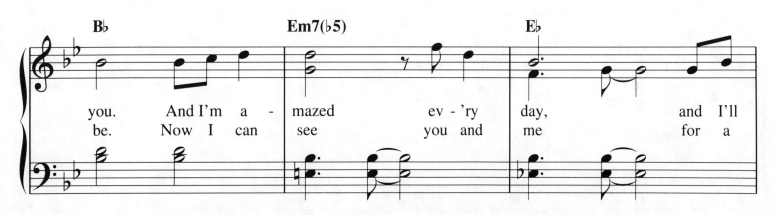

you. And I'm a - mazed ev-'ry day, and I'll
be. Now I can see you and me for a

© Copyright 1986 by MCA MUSIC PUBLISHING, A Division of UNIVERSAL STUDIOS, INC.,
CHRISWALD MUSIC, INC., HOPI SOUND MUSIC, WARNER-TAMERLANE PUBLISHING CORP., FLAMINGO ROSE MUSIC and CHOY LA RUE MUSIC
All Rights for CHRISWALD MUSIC, INC. and HOPI SOUND MUSIC Controlled and Administered by MCA MUSIC PUBLISHING, A Division of UNIVERSAL STUDIOS, INC.
All Rights for FLAMINGO ROSE MUSIC and CHOY LA RUE MUSIC Administered by WARNER-TAMERLANE PUBLISHING CORP.
International Copyright Secured   All Rights Reserved
MCA music publishing

need you ____
life - time. ___
'til all the moun-tains are
Un - til the last moon is

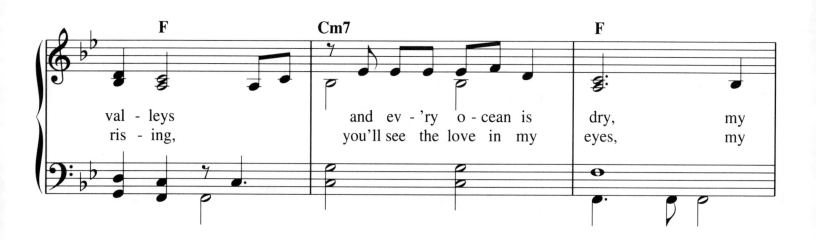

val - leys
ris - ing,
and ev - 'ry o - cean is
you'll see the love in my
dry, my
eyes, my

love.
love.
I'll be yours un-til the
sun does-n't shine, __ 'til

time stands still, __
un - til the winds __ don't
blow. When to - day is just a

I'LL BE LOVING YOU
(Forever)

Words and Music by
MAURICE STARR

I'm not that kind of guy who can take a bro-ken heart, __ so don't
I count the bless-ings _____ that keep our love new. _____ There's

© 1988 EMI APRIL MUSIC INC. and MAURICE STARR MUSIC
All Rights Controlled and Administered by EMI APRIL MUSIC INC.
All Rights Reserved   International Copyright Secured   Used by Permission

ev - er leave.___ I don't want to see us part. The ver - y thought of
one for me,___ and a mil - lion ___ for ___ you. There's just so much that

los - ing you means___ that ev - 'ry - thing___ would
I want to say.___ But when I look at you ___

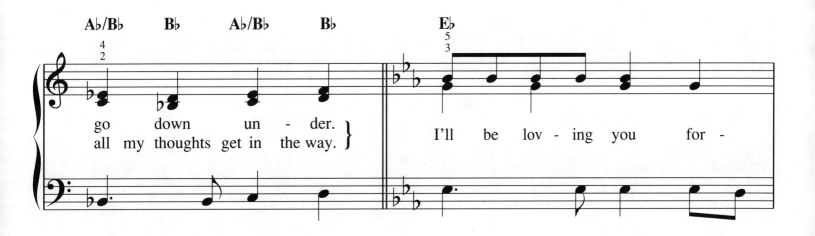

go down un - der.
all my thoughts get in the way. } I'll be lov - ing you for -

ev - er, ___ just as long as you want me to be.___

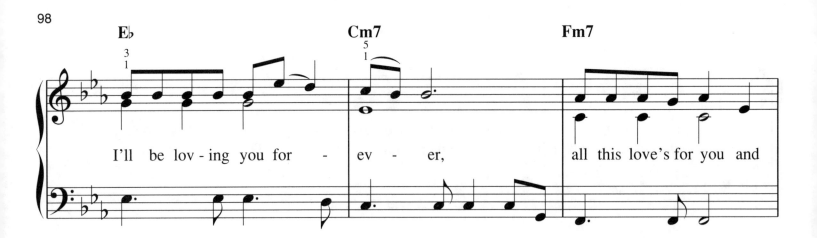

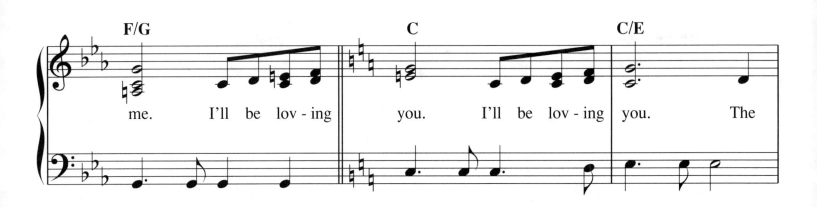

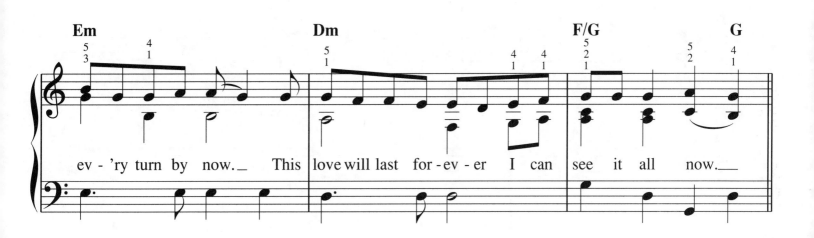

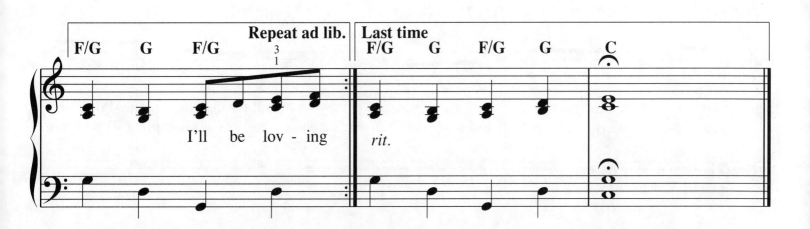

I'LL MAKE LOVE TO YOU

Words and Music by
BABYFACE

Copyright © 1994 Sony/ATV Songs LLC and ECAF Music
All Rights Administered by Sony/ATV Music Publishing, 8 Music Square West, Nashville, TN 37203
International Copyright Secured   All Rights Reserved

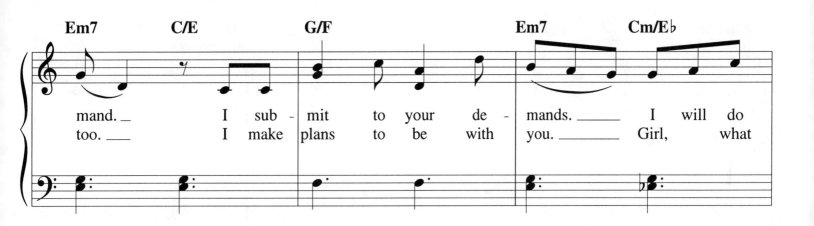

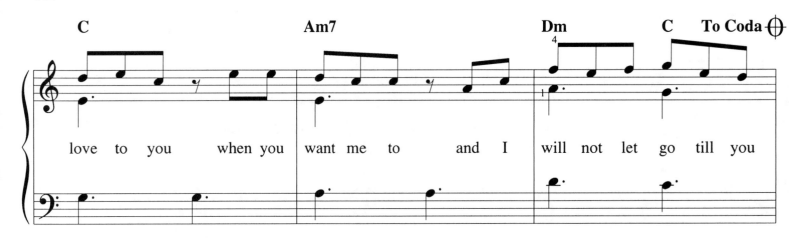

love to you when you want me to and I will not let go till you

tell me to. _____ Girl, re - tell me to. Ba - by, to -

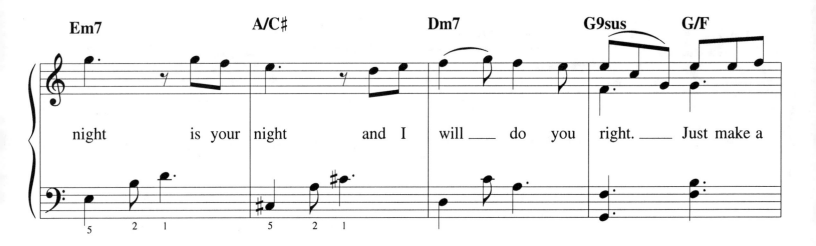

night is your night and I will __ do you right. __ Just make a

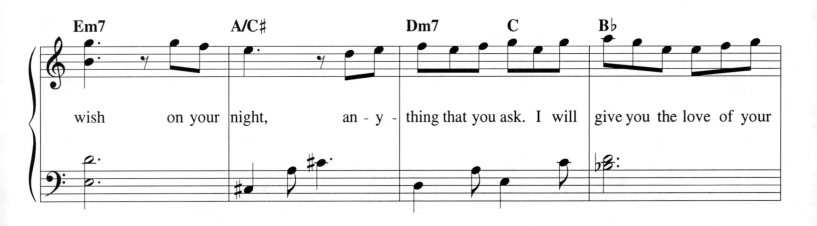

wish on your night, an - y - thing that you ask. I will give you the love of your

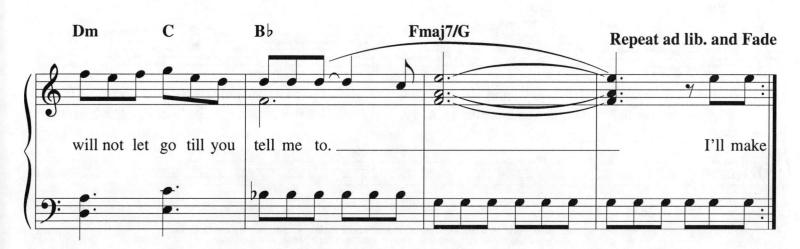

IF I EVER FALL IN LOVE

Words and Music by
CARL MARTIN

Slowly

Ooh da da doop do doop. Ooh da da doop do doop. Ooh da da doop do doop.

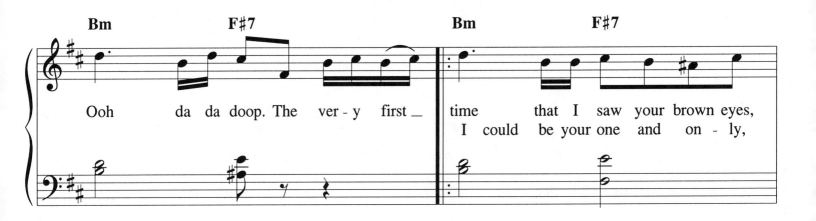

Ooh da da doop. The ver-y first ___ time that I saw your brown eyes,
I could be your one and on - ly,

your lips said, "Hel - lo" and I said "Hi". I knew right then you were the
prom-ise that you'll nev-er leave me lone - ly. I just want to be the one you

© Copyright 1992 by MUSIC CORPORATION OF AMERICA, INC., GASOLINE ALLEY MUSIC and CAMEO APPEARANCE BY RAMSES
All Rights Controlled and Administered by MUSIC CORPORATION OF AMERICA, INC.
International Copyright Secured   All Rights Reserved
MCA music publishing

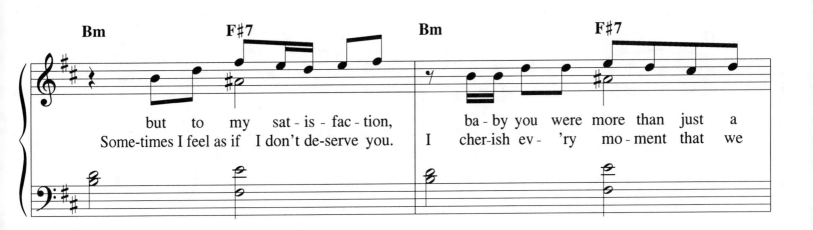

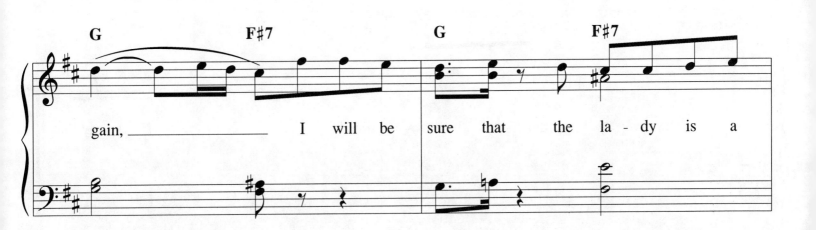

friend. And if I ev... ev - er fall in love so

true, _____ I will be sure that the la - dy's just like you. _____ Oh.

Ooh da da doop da doop. Ooh da da doop do doop.

The ver - y next time she'll be my friend. If I say that

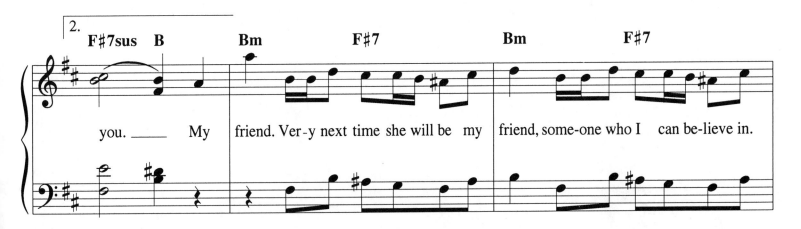

2.

F#7sus B   Bm   F#7   Bm   F#7

you. ___ My friend. Ver-y next time she will be my friend, some-one who I can be-lieve in.

Bm   F#7   Bm   F#7

Ver - y next time she will be my friend, some-one who I can be-lieve in.

Bm   F#7   Bm   F#7

Ver - y next time she will be my friend, some-one who I can be-lieve in.

Bm   F#7   Bm   D.S. al Coda   CODA   F#7sus   B

Ver-y next time she will be my friend. And if I   you. ___

IF I EVER LOSE MY FAITH IN YOU

Words and Music by
STING

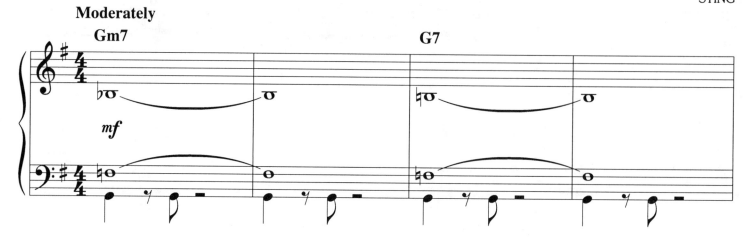

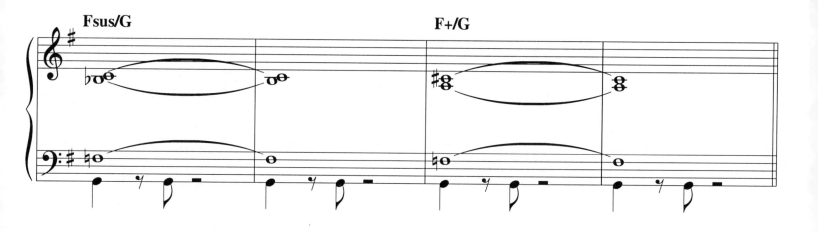

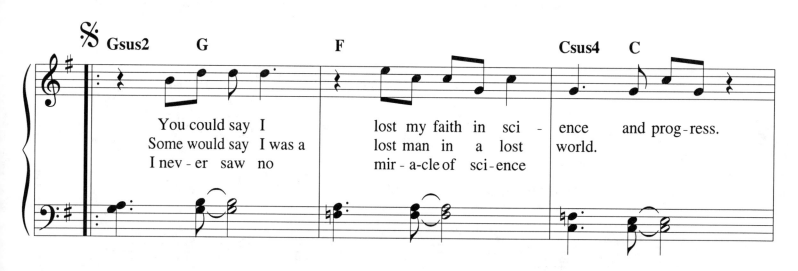

You could say I   lost my faith in sci - ence   and prog - ress.
Some would say I was a lost man in a lost world.
I nev - er saw no   mir - a - cle of sci - ence

Copyright © 1992 Gordon M. Sumner Represented by Magnetic Publishing Ltd. (PRS)
Represented by Reggatta Music Ltd. (BMI) and Administered by Irving Music, Inc. (BMI) in the U.S. and Canada
International Copyright Secured   All Rights Reserved

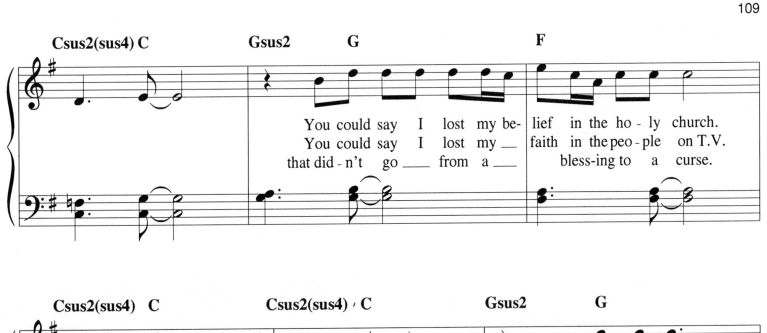

You could say   I   lost my be- lief   in the ho - ly   church.
You could say   I   lost my ___ faith   in the peo - ple   on T.V.
that did - n't   go ___ from a ___   bless-ing to   a   curse.

You could   say   I
You could   say   I lost my be -
I nev - er   saw   no

To Coda ⊕

lost my sense of di-rec – tion.
lief in our pol-i-ti – cians.
mil-i-tar-y sol – u-tion

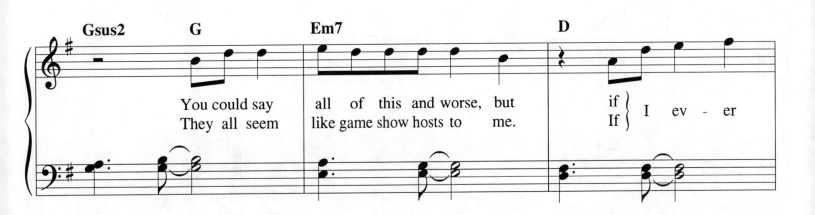

You could say   all of this and worse, but   if } I   ev - er
They all seem   like game show hosts to   me.   If }

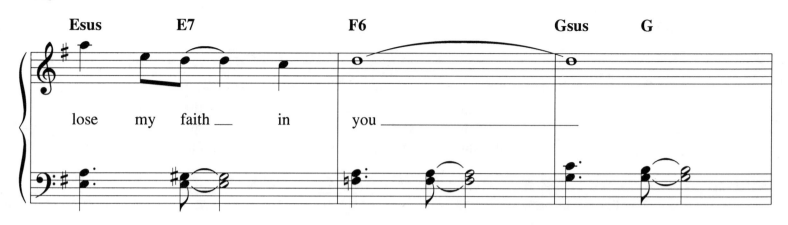

lose   my   faith ___   in   you _____

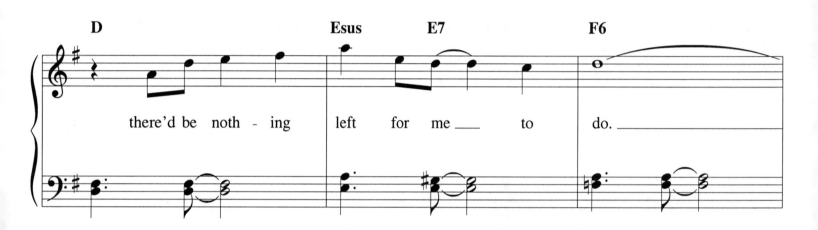

there'd be noth - ing   left   for   me ___   to   do. _____

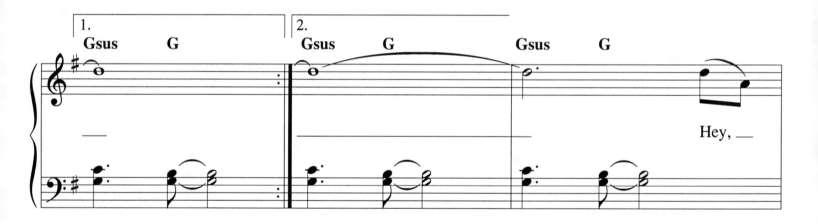

___   Hey, ___

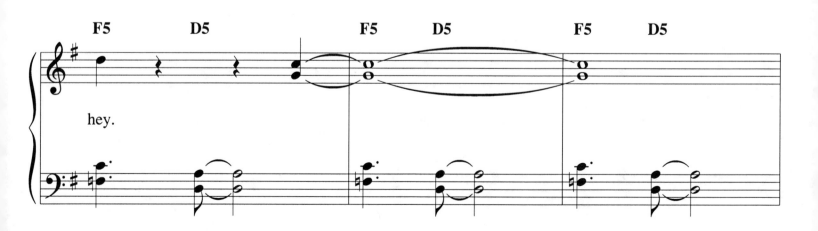

hey.

I could be lost in - side their

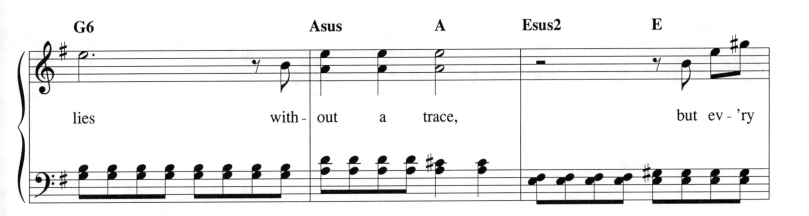

lies with - out a trace, but ev - 'ry

D.S. al Coda

time I close my eyes I see your face.

CODA

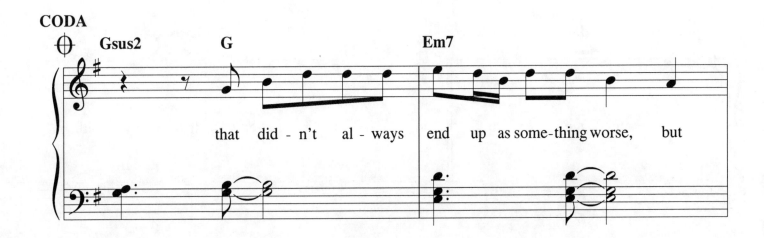

that did - n't al - ways end up as some-thing worse, but

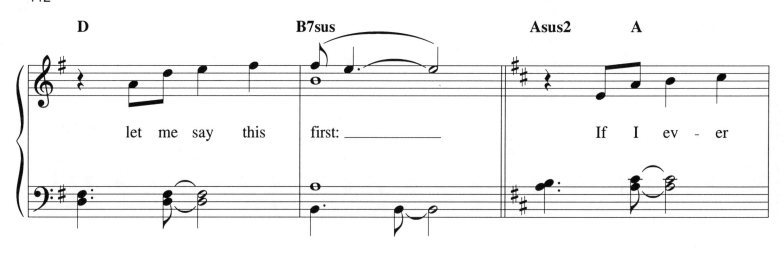

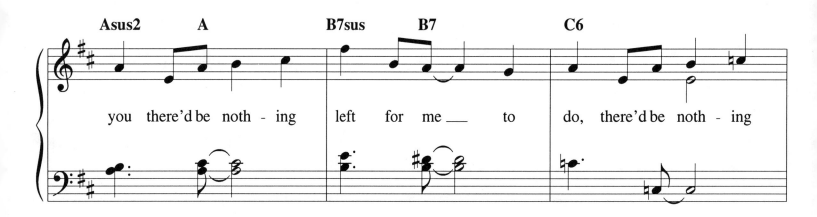

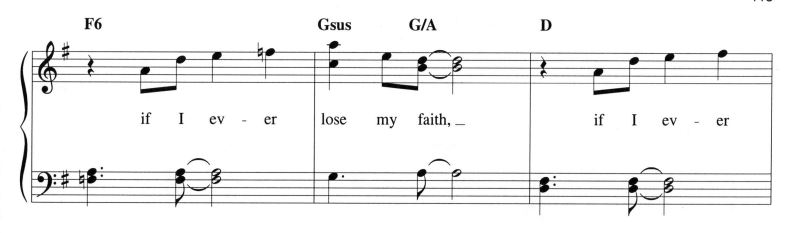

if I ev – er lose my faith, _ if I ev – er

lose my faith, _ if I ev – er lose my faith _

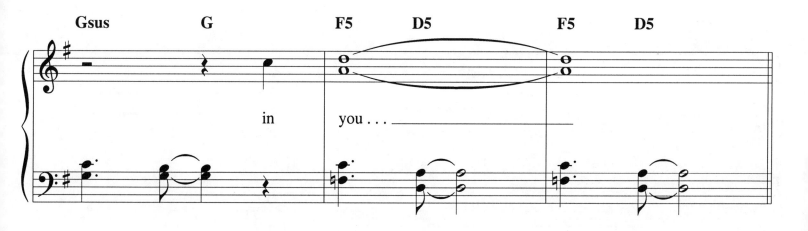

in you . . . _

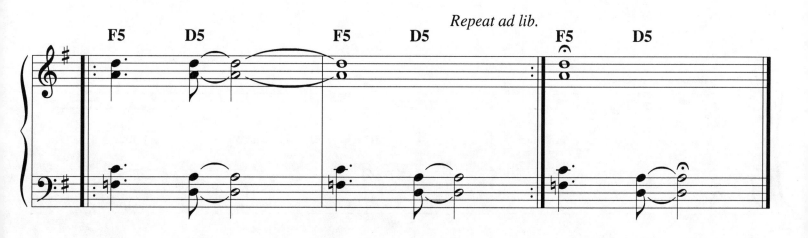

Repeat ad lib.

IF I NEVER KNEW YOU

(Love Theme from POCAHONTAS)
from Walt Disney's POCAHONTAS

Music by ALAN MENKEN
Lyrics by STEPHEN SCHWARTZ

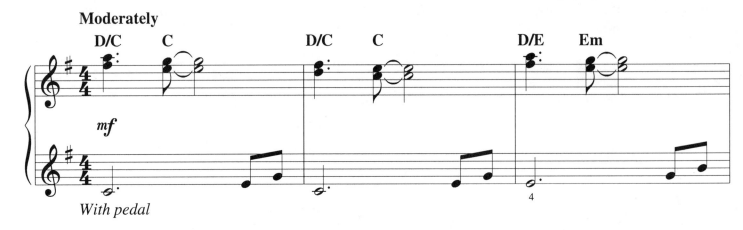

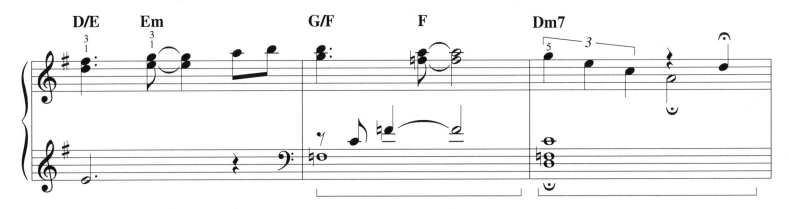

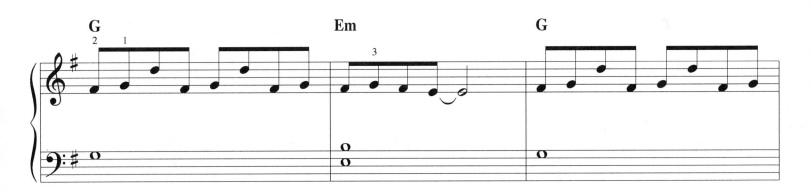

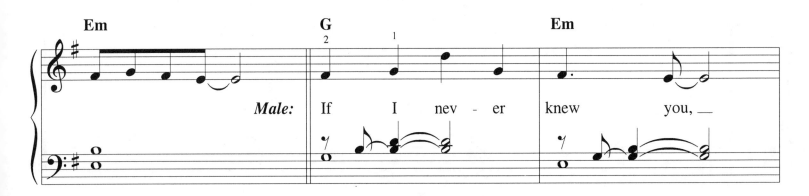

Male: If I nev-er knew you, ___

© 1995 Wonderland Music Company, Inc. and Walt Disney Music Company
International Copyright Secured   All Rights Reserved

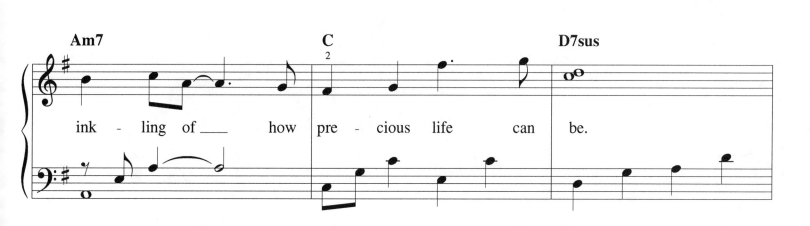

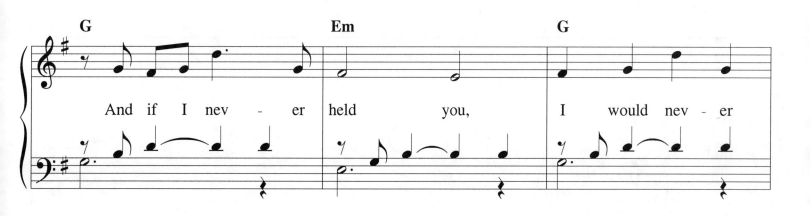

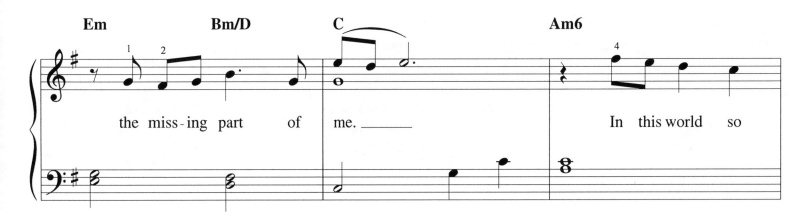

the miss-ing part of me. _____ In this world so

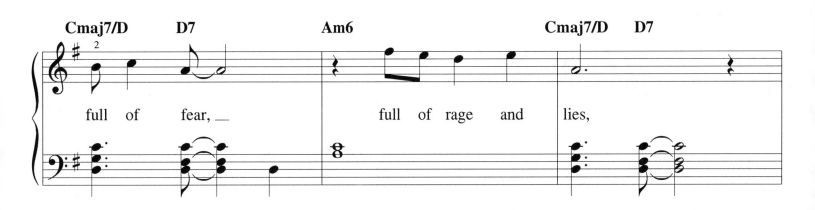

full of fear, _ full of rage and lies,

I can see _ the truth so clear _ in your eyes, _ so

dry your eyes. _ And I'm so grate - ful to you.

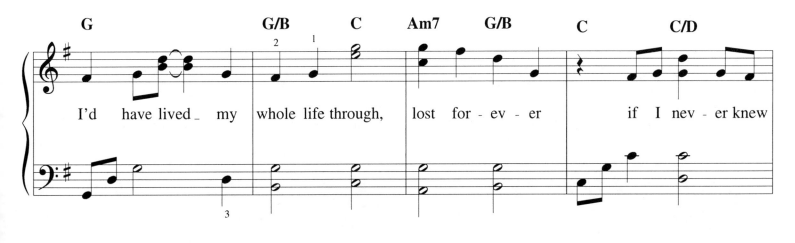

I'd have lived_ my whole life through, lost for-ev-er if I nev-er knew

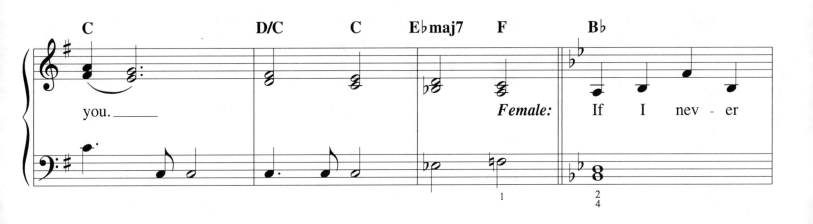

you._____ *Female:* If I nev-er

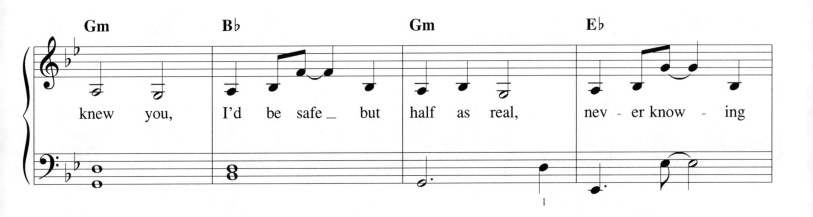

knew you, I'd be safe_ but half as real, nev-er know-ing

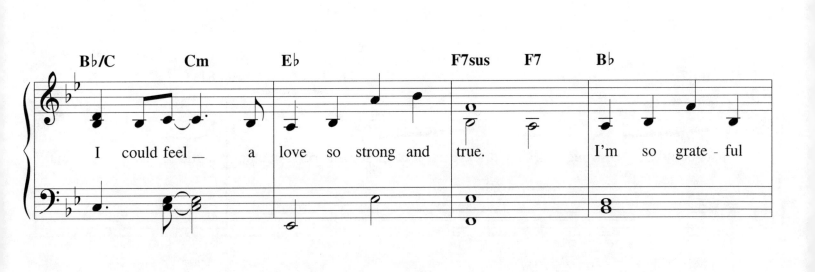

I could feel _ a love so strong and true. I'm so grate-ful

Gm   Bb   Bb/D   Eb   Cm7   Bb/D

to you.   I'd have lived my   whole life through,   lost for - ev - er

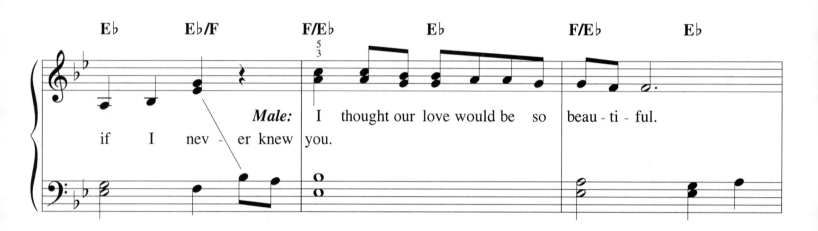

Eb   Eb/F   F/Eb   Eb   F/Eb   Eb

if   I   nev - er knew you.   *Male:* I   thought our love would be   so   beau - ti - ful.

Dm7   Gm

Female: Some - how we'd make the whole world   bright. __   *Both:* I   nev - er knew that fear and

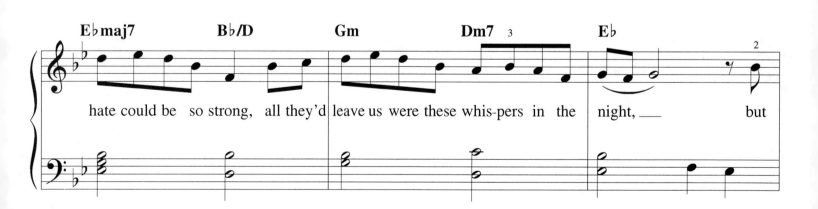

Ebmaj7   Bb/D   Gm   Dm7   Eb

hate could be   so strong,   all they'd leave us were these whis-pers in the   night, ___   but

still my heart is say-ing we were right.___ *Female:* Oh._____

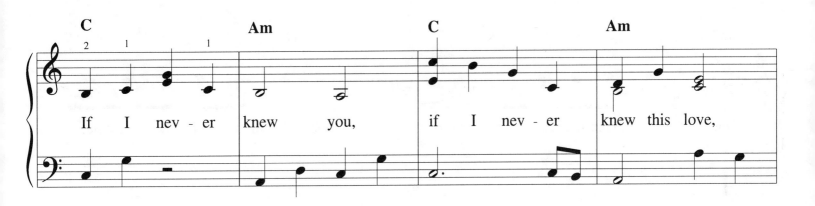

If I nev-er knew you, if I nev-er knew this love,

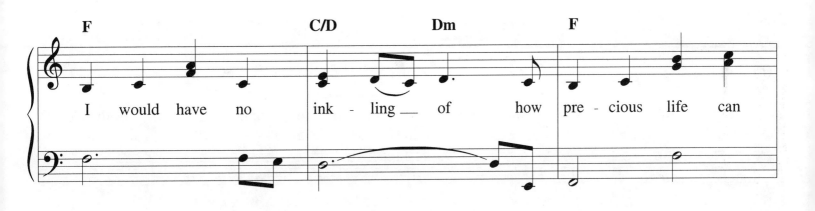

I would have no ink-ling __ of how pre-cious life can

be.

Both: I thought our love would be so beau-ti-ful,

some-how we'd make the whole world bright. ___ Female: I thought our love would be so

beau-ti-ful, we'd turn the dark-ness in-to light. ___ Both: And

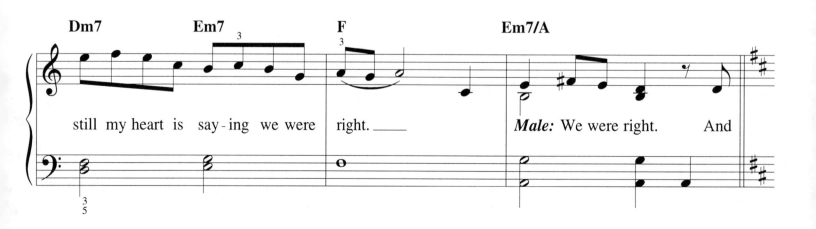

still my heart is say-ing we were right. ___ Male: We were right. And

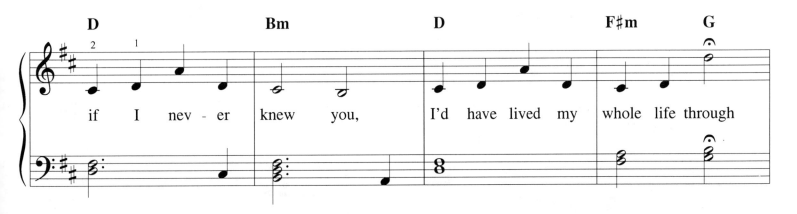

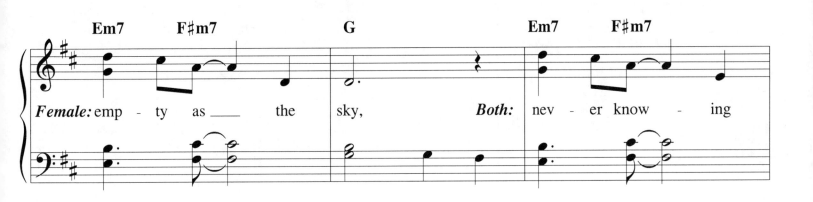

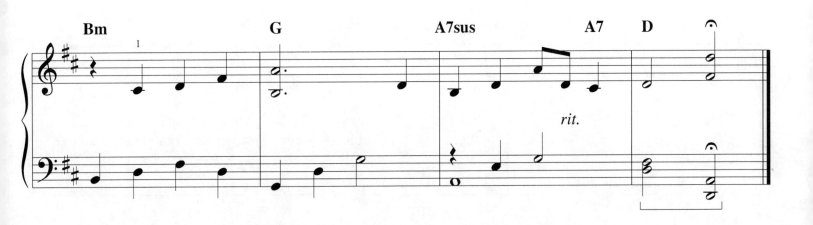

IF WE HOLD ON TOGETHER
from THE LAND BEFORE TIME

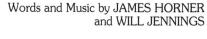

Words and Music by JAMES HORNER
and WILL JENNINGS

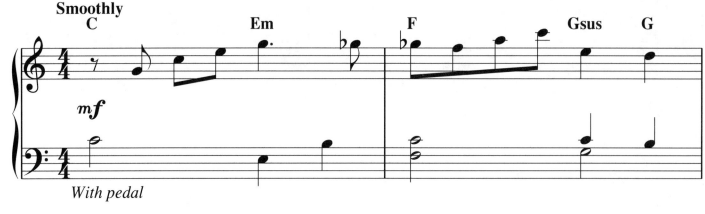

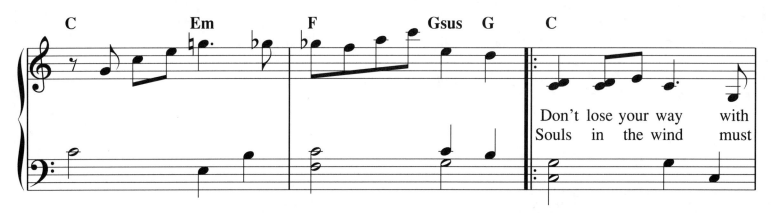

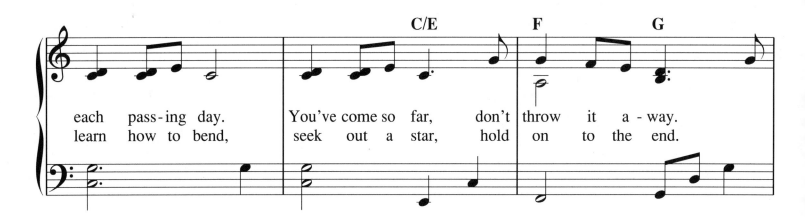

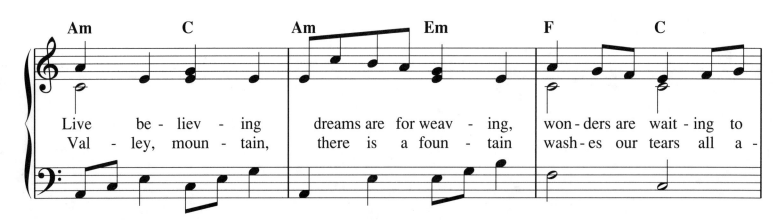

Don't lose your way   with
Souls in the wind   must

each pass-ing day.   You've come so far,   don't throw it a - way.
learn how to bend,   seek out a star,   hold on to the end.

Live be - liev - ing   dreams are for weav - ing,   won - ders are wait - ing to
Val - ley, moun - tain,   there is a foun - tain   wash - es our tears all a -

© Copyright 1988 by MCA MUSIC PUBLISHING, A Division of UNIVERSAL STUDIOS, INC.
International Copyright Secured   All Rights Reserved

MCA music publishing

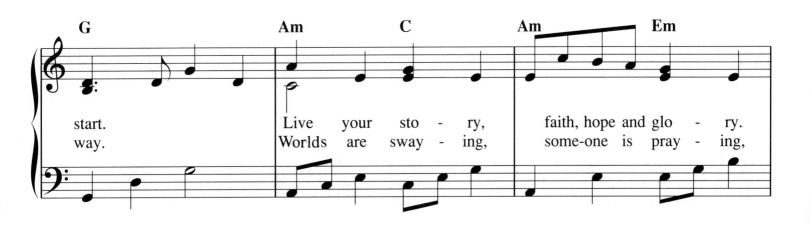

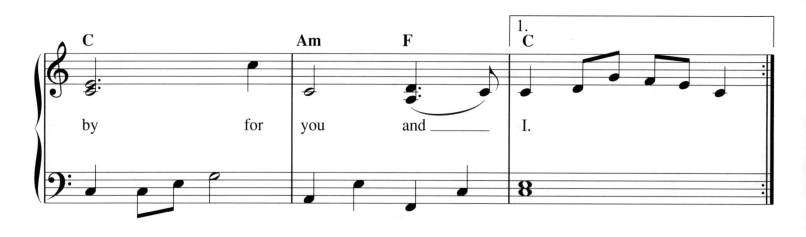

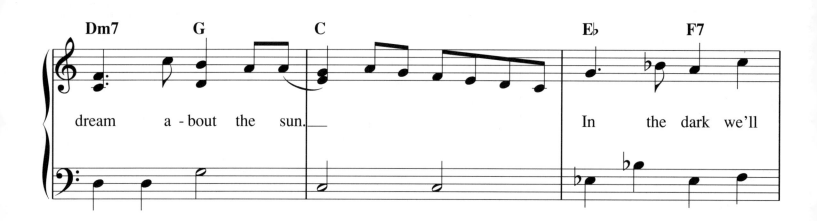

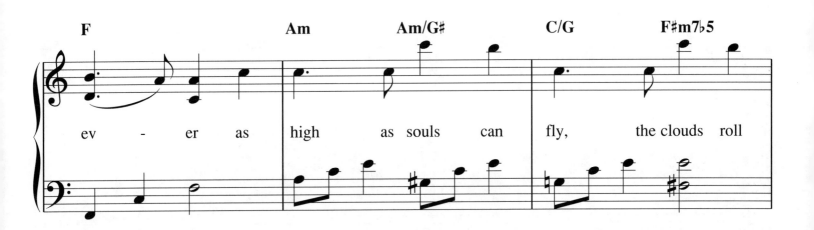

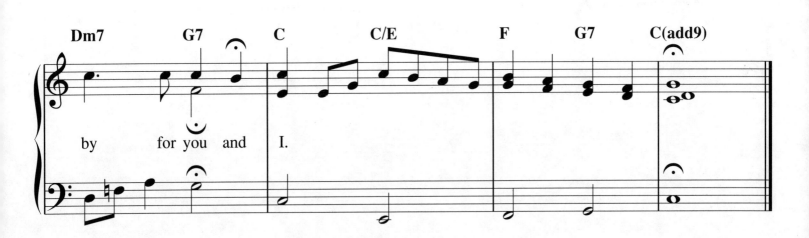

LOST IN YOUR EYES

Words and Music by
DEBORAH GIBSON

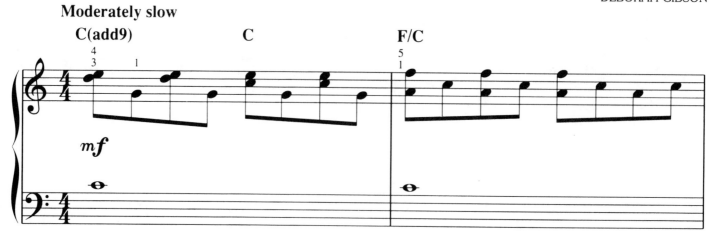

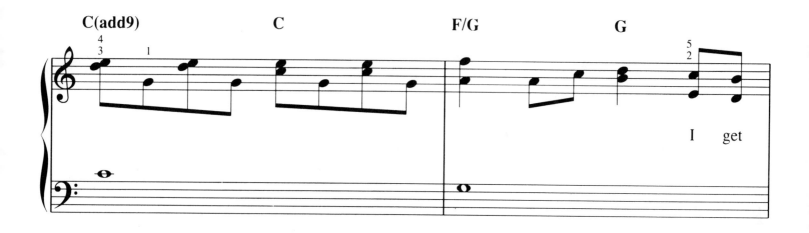

I get

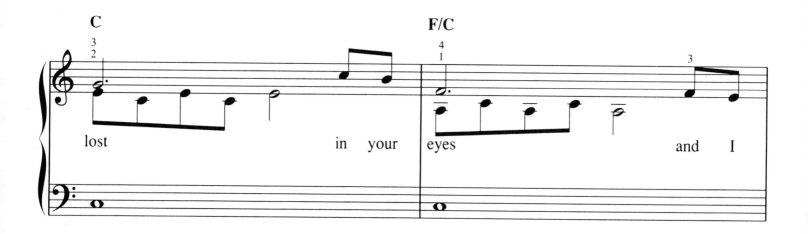

lost   in   your eyes   and   I

Copyright © 1988 Deborah Ann's Music, Inc. and Walden Music, Inc. (ASCAP)
International Copyright Secured   All Rights Reserved

feel _____ my spir - its rise and soar like the

wind. Is it love that I am ___

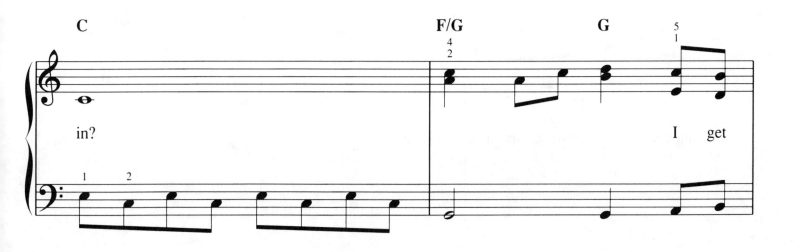

in? I get

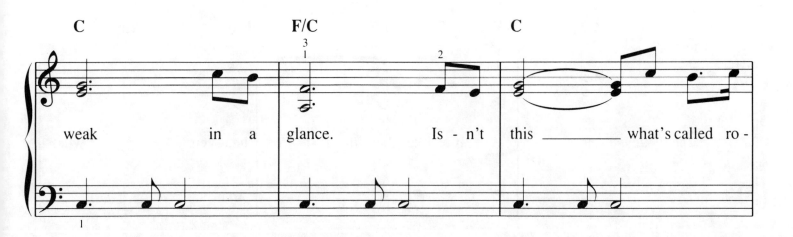

weak in a glance. Is - n't this _____ what's called ro -

128

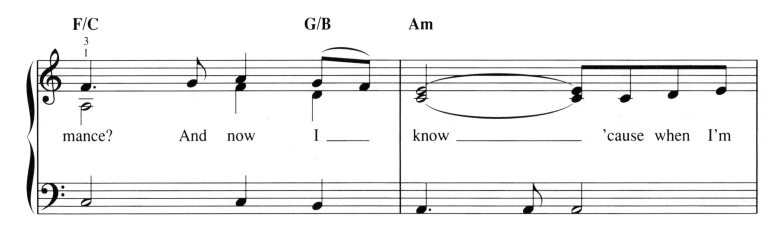

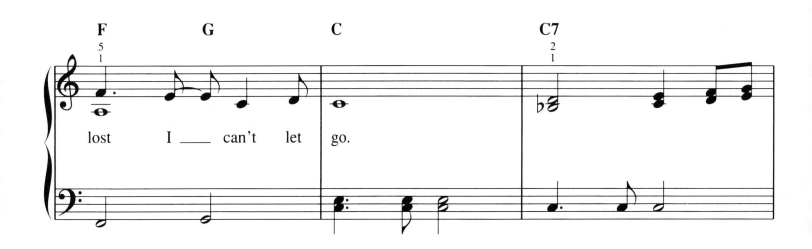

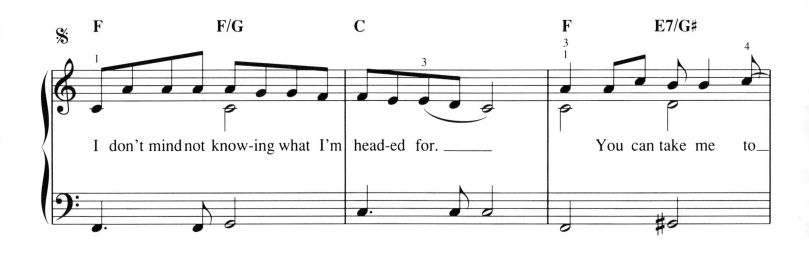

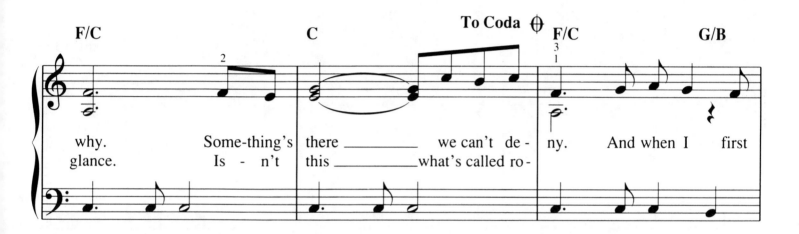

va - tion _____ seems worlds a - way, oh I'll ___ be found _____ when I am

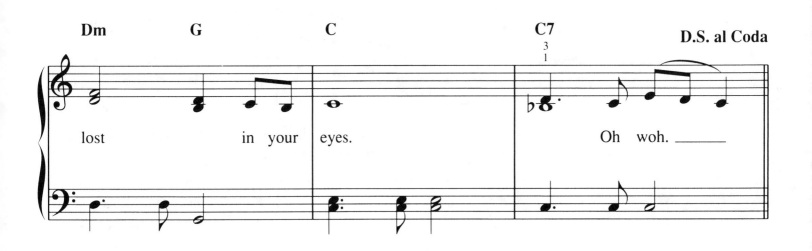

lost in your eyes. Oh woh. _____

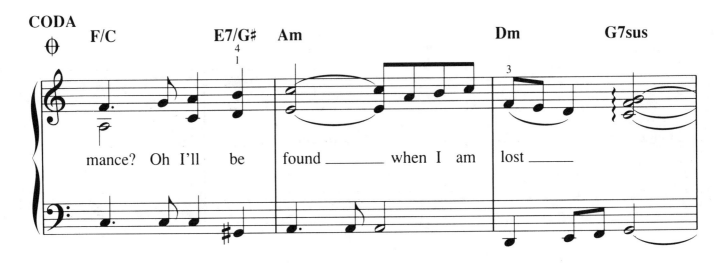

mance? Oh I'll be found _____ when I am lost _____

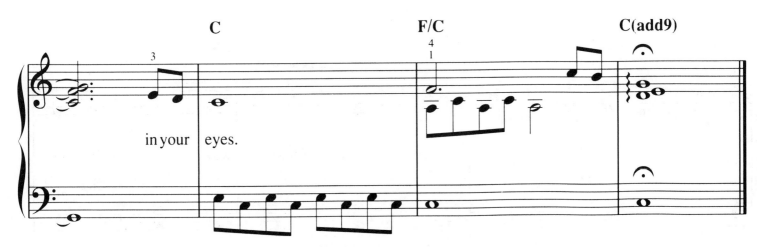

in your eyes.

THE POWER OF LOVE

Words by MARY SUSAN APPLEGATE and JENNIFER RUSH
Music by CANDY DEROUGE and GUNTHER MENDE

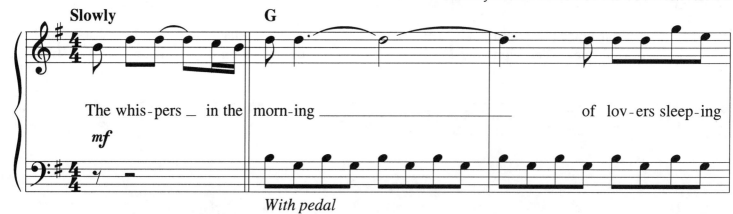

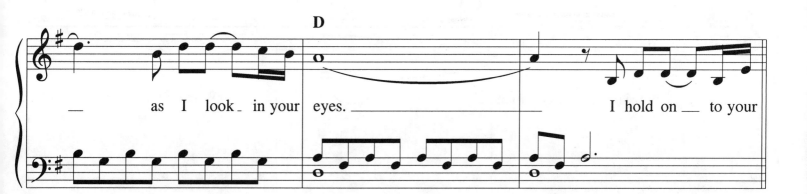

© 1986 EMI SONGS MUSIKVERLAG GMBH
All Rights for the U.S.A. and Canada Controlled and Administered by EMI APRIL MUSIC INC.
All Rights Reserved   International Copyright Secured   Used by Permission

132

LOVE OF A LIFETIME

Words and Music by BILL LEVERTY
and CARL SNARE

Copyright © 1990 Sony/ATV Tunes LLC and Wocka Wocka Music
All Rights Administered by Sony/ATV Music Publishing, 8 Music Square West, Nashville, TN 37203
International Copyright Secured   All Rights Reserved

137

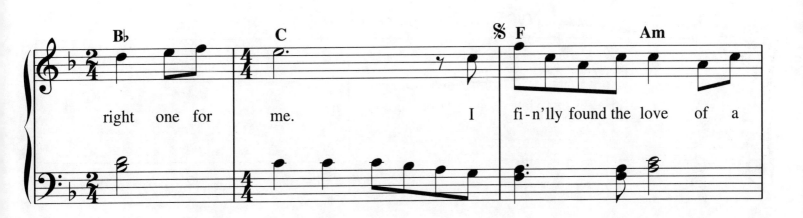

life-time, a love to last my whole life through. I

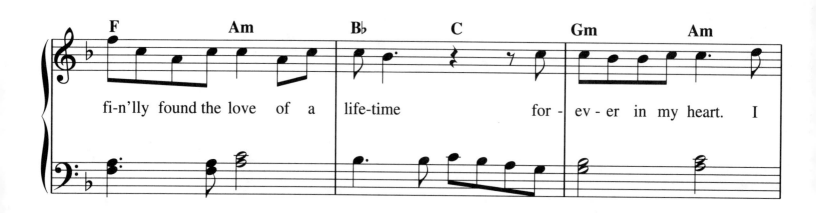

fi-n'lly found the love of a life-time for - ev - er in my heart. I

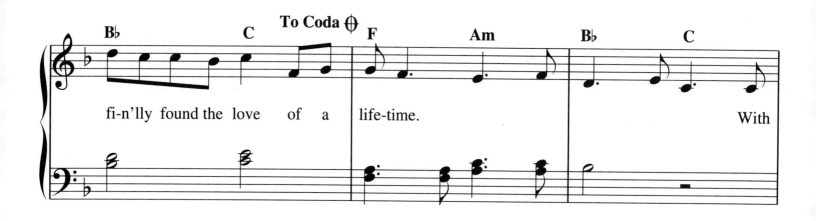

To Coda

fi-n'lly found the love of a life-time. With

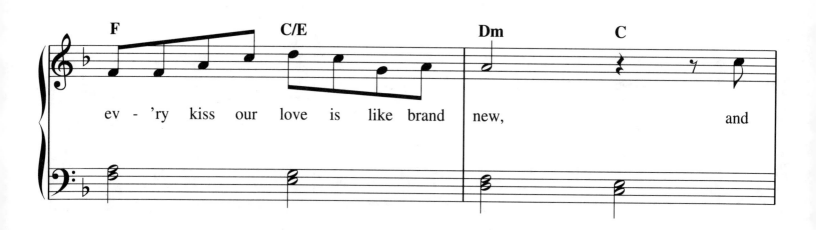

ev - 'ry kiss our love is like brand new, and

ev - 'ry star up in the sky was made for me and you.

Still, we both know that the road is long, but we

D.S. al Coda

know we'll be to-geth-er be - cause our love is strong. I

CODA

life-time.

LOVE TAKES TIME

Words and Music by MARIAH CAREY
and BEN MARGULIES

Copyright © 1990 Vision Of Love Songs, Inc. and Been Jammin' Music
All Rights on behalf of Vision Of Love Songs, Inc. Administered by Sony/ATV Music Publishing, 8 Music Square West, Nashville, TN 37203
International Copyright Secured   All Rights Reserved

Love takes time to heal when you're hurt-ing so___ much. Could-n't see that

I ___ was blind ___ to let you ___ go. ___ I can't es- cape the

pain ___ in - side ___ 'cause love ___ takes ___ time.

I don't want to be here. I don't want to be ___ here ___ a -

142

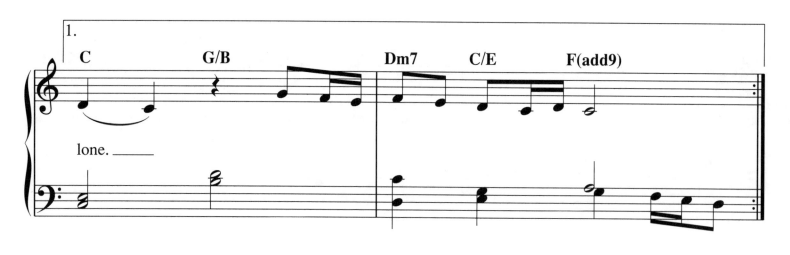

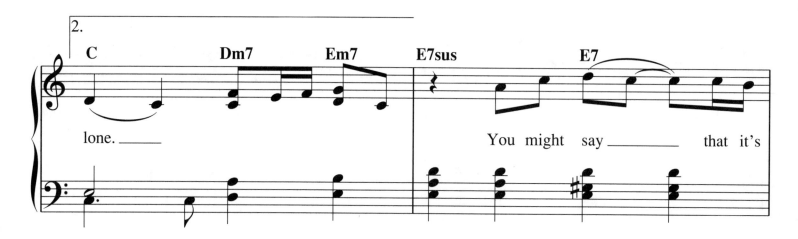

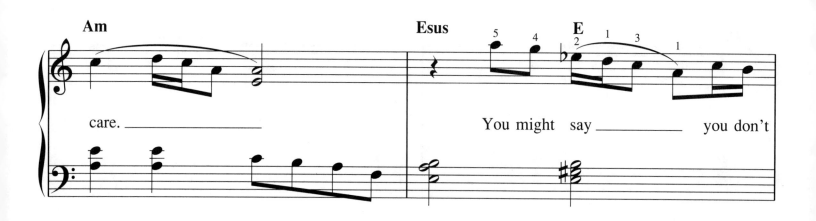

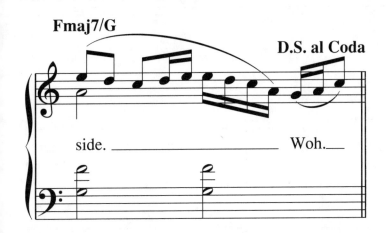

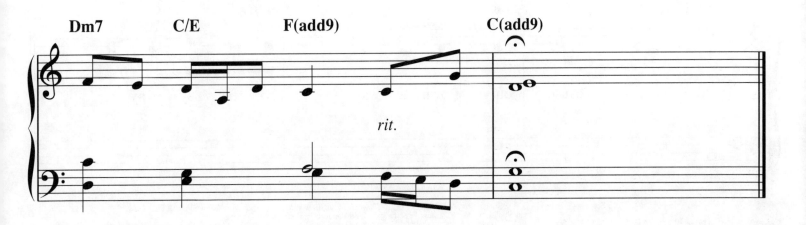

ONE SWEET DAY

Words and Music by MARIAH CAREY, WALTER AFANASIEFF, SHAWN STOCKMAN,
MICHAEL McCARY, NATHAN MORRIS and WANYA MORRIS

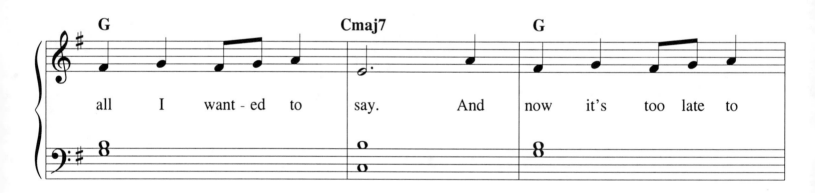

Copyright © 1995 Sony/ATV Songs LLC, Rye Songs, Sony/ATV Tunes LLC, Wallyworld Music, Ensign Music Corporation, Shawn Patrick Publishing,
Aynaw Publishing, Black Panther Publishing Co. and Vanderpool Publishing
All Rights on behalf of Sony/ATV Songs LLC, Rye Songs, Sony/ATV Tunes LLC and Wallyworld Music Administered by Sony/ATV Music Publishing, 8 Music Square West, Nashville, TN 37203
International Copyright Secured   All Rights Reserved

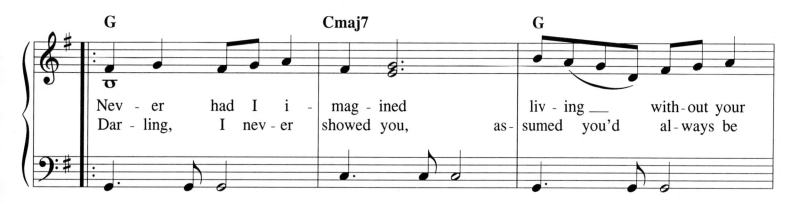

Never had I i - mag - ined liv - ing ___ with-out your
Dar - ling, I nev - er showed you, as- sumed you'd al -ways be

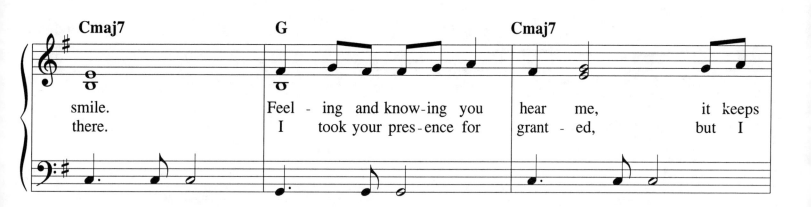

smile.
there. Feel - ing and know-ing you hear me, it keeps
I took your pres -ence for grant - ed, but I

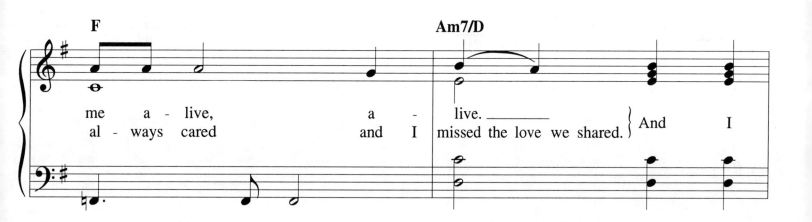

me a - live, a - live. ___ missed the love we shared. } And I
al - ways cared and I

know you're shin - ing down on me from heav - en like so

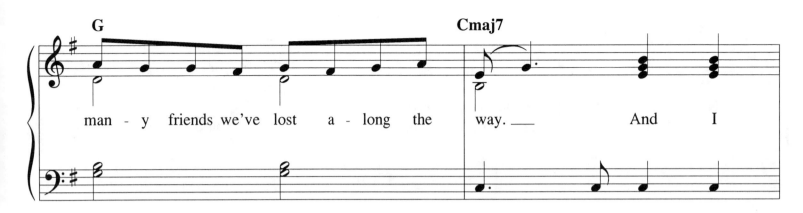

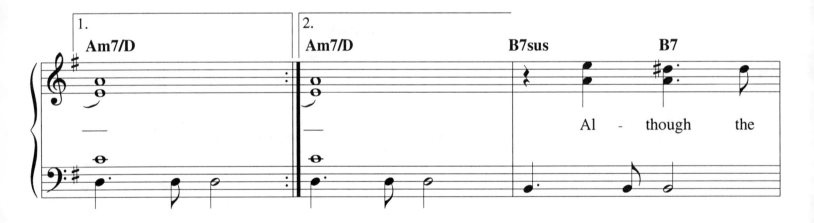

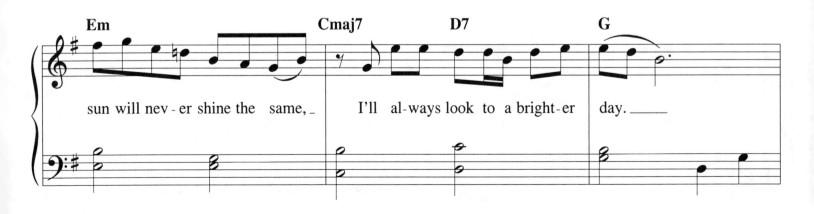

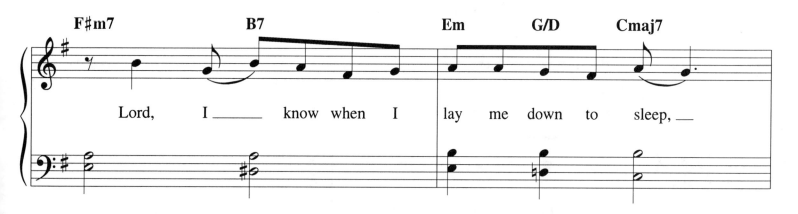

Lord, I _____ know when I lay me down to sleep, __

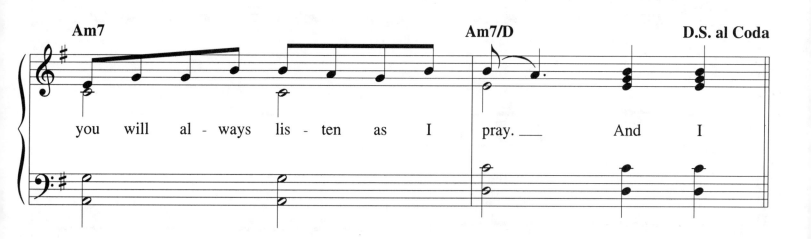

you will al - ways lis - ten as I pray. __ And I

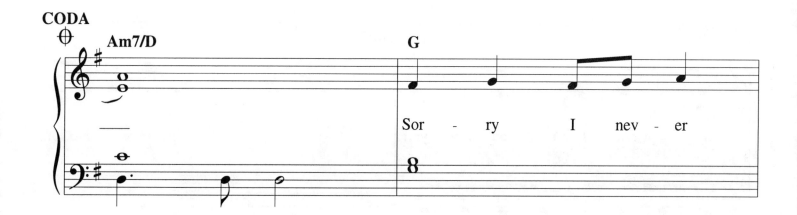

CODA

_____ Sor - ry I nev - er

told you all I want - ed to say.

REAL LOVE

Words and Music by
JOHN LENNON

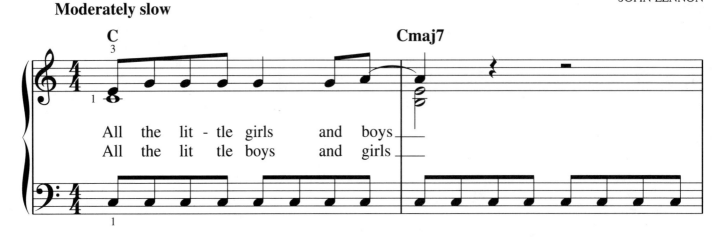

All the lit - tle girls and boys
All the lit - tle boys and girls

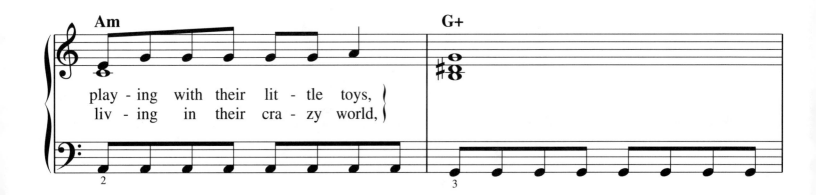

play - ing with their lit - tle toys,
liv - ing in their cra - zy world,

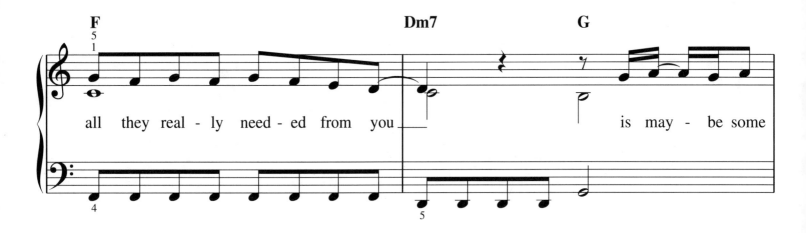

all they real - ly need - ed from you _____ is may - be some

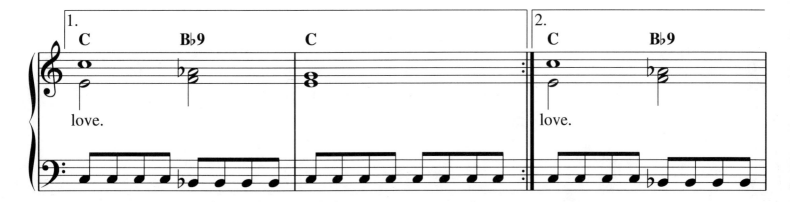

love.

love.

Copyright © 1988, 1996 Lenono Music
All Rights Administered by Sony/ATV Music Publishing, 8 Music Square West, Nashville, TN 37203
International Copyright Secured   All Rights Reserved

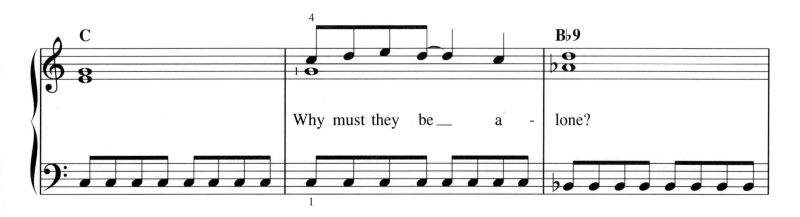

Why must they be a - lone?

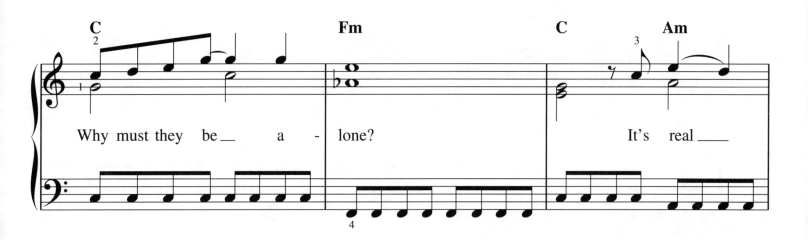

Why must they be a - lone?   It's real ___

life.   Yes, it's real _____

whistle

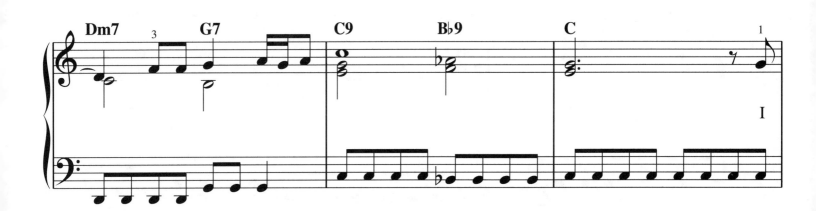

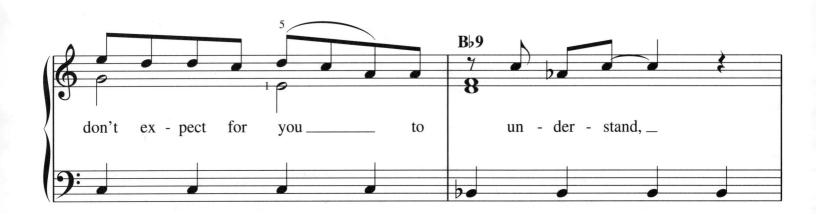

don't ex - pect for you _____ to un - der - stand, _

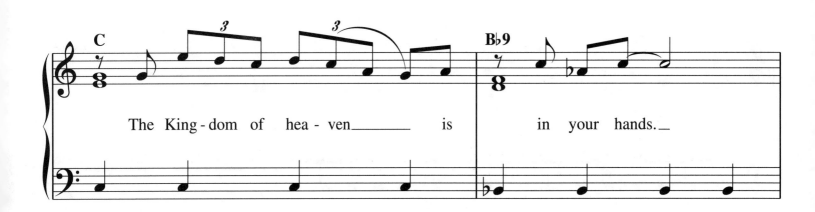

The King - dom of hea - ven _____ is in your hands. _

I don't ex-pect you _____ to wake from your dream._

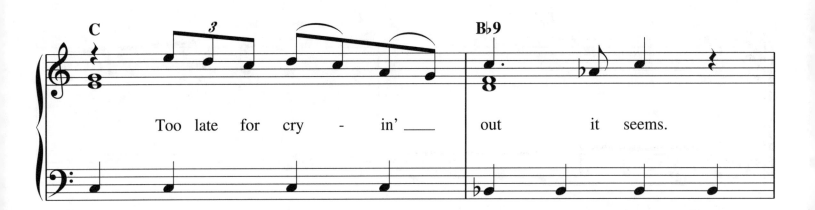

Too late for cry - in' ____ out it seems.

All the lit-tle plans and schemes____

noth-ing but a bunch of dreams.____

All you real-ly need-ed to do _____ is may-be some

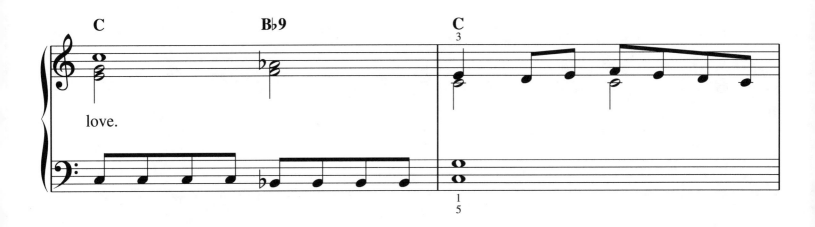

love.

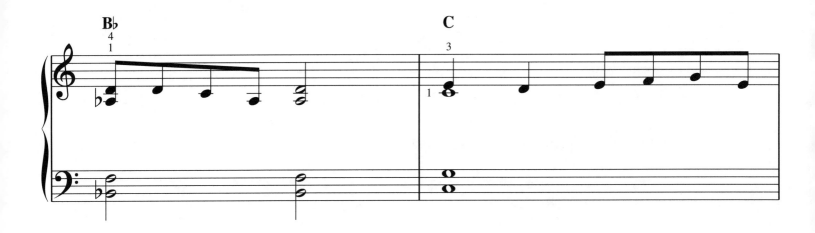

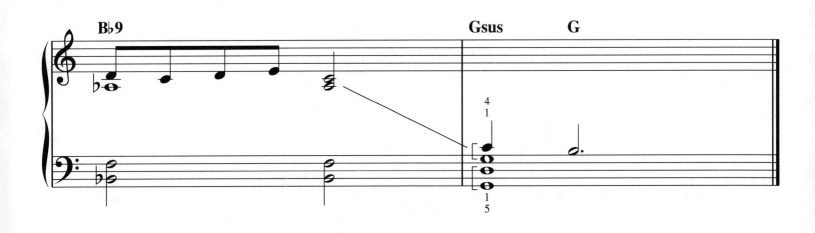

SAVE THE BEST FOR LAST

Words and Music by PHIL GALDSTON,
JON LIND and WENDY WALDMAN

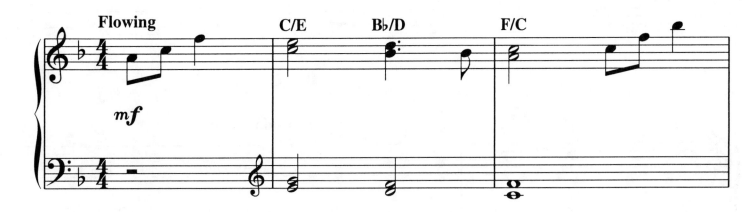

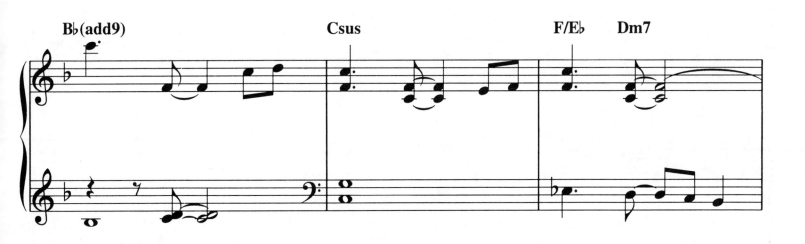

Some-times the | snow comes down_ in June. Some-times the
nights you came_ to me when some sil - ly
snow comes down_ in June. Some-times the

Copyright © 1989 PolyGram International Publishing, Inc., Kazzoom Music Inc., EMI Virgin Songs, Inc., Big Mystique Music,
Windswept Pacific Entertainment Co. d/b/a Longitude Music Co. and Moon And Stars Music
All Rights for Big Mystique Music Controlled and Administered by EMI Virgin Songs, Inc.
International Copyright Secured   All Rights Reserved

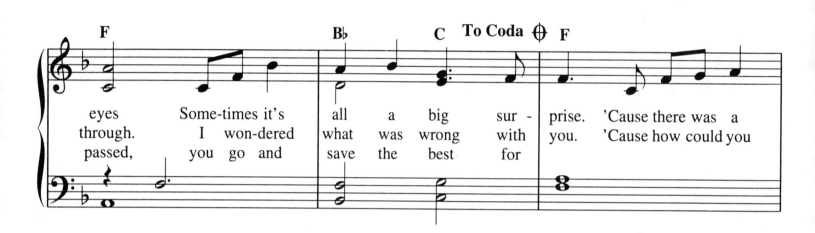

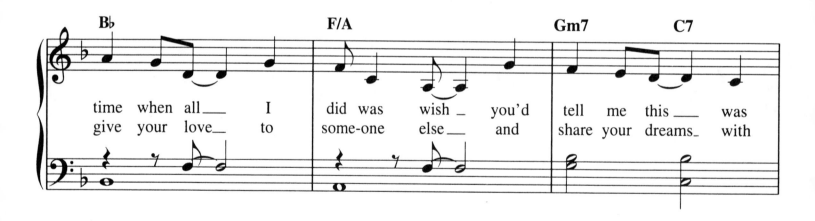

somehow it's e-nough. And now we're stand-ing face __ to
one thing you can't see. But now we're stand-ing face __ to

face. / face. } Isn't this world a cra-zy place? Just when I

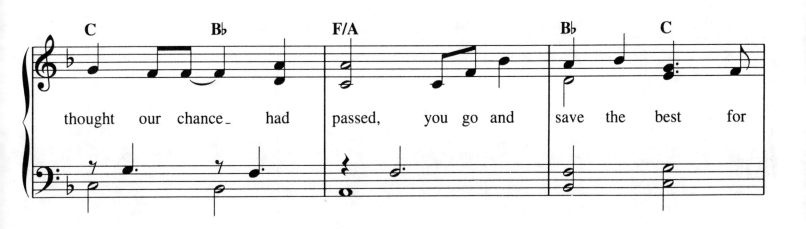

thought our chance __ had passed, you go and save the best for

1.
last.

All of the last.

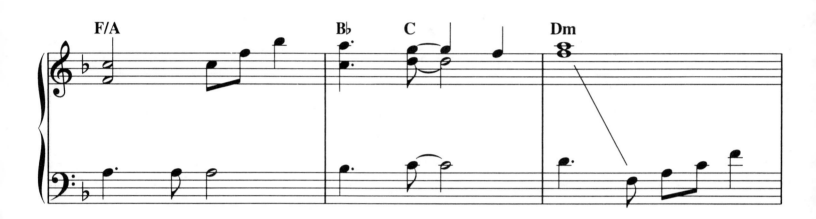

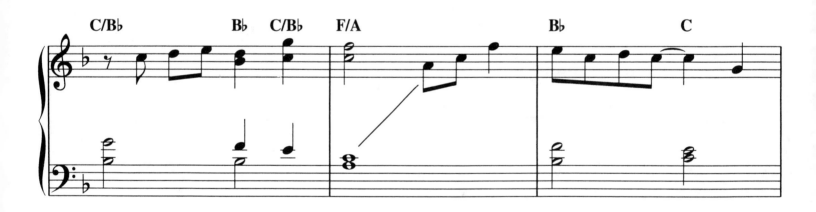

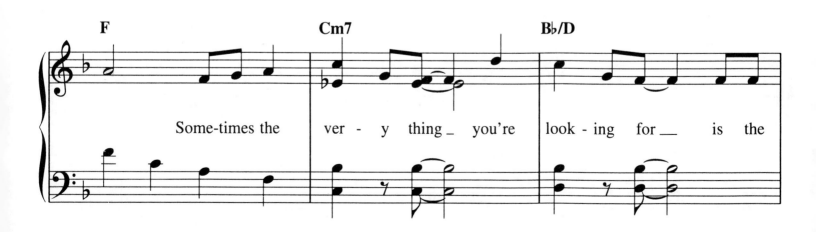

Some-times the ver - y thing _ you're look - ing for _ is the

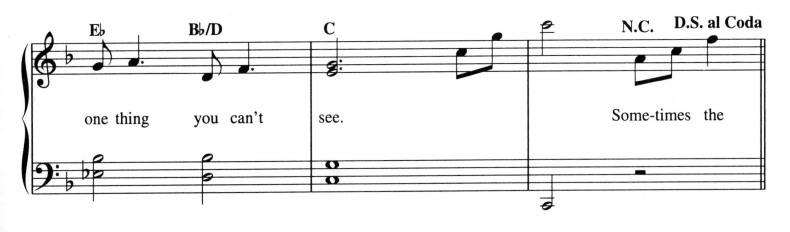

one thing   you can't   see.   Some-times the

last.

You went and   saved the   best   for   last.

SAVING ALL MY LOVE FOR YOU

Words by GERRY GOFFIN
Music by MICHAEL MASSER

© 1978 SCREEN GEMS-EMI MUSIC INC., LAUREN-WESLEY MUSIC INC. and PRINCE STREET MUSIC
All Rights for LAUREN-WESLEY MUSIC INC. Controlled and Administered by SCREEN GEMS-EMI MUSIC INC.
All Rights Reserved   International Copyright Secured   Used by Permission

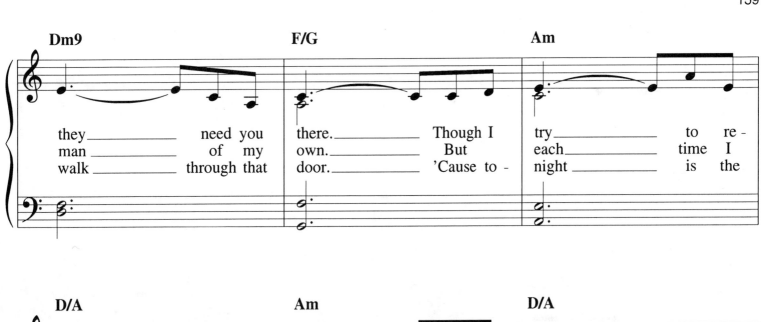

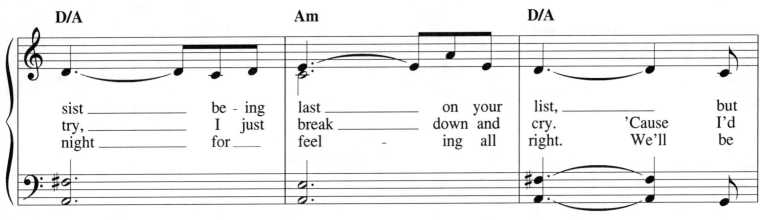

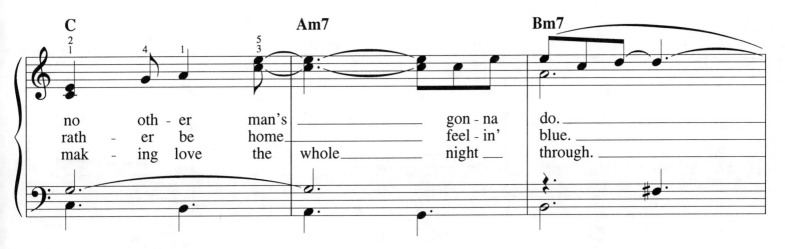

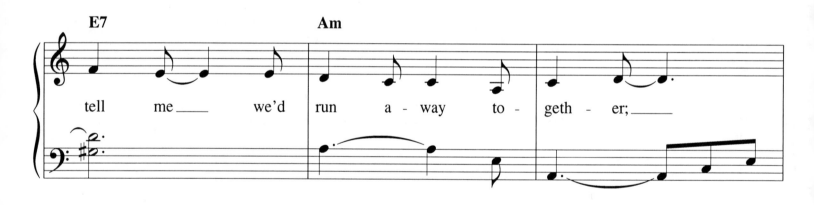

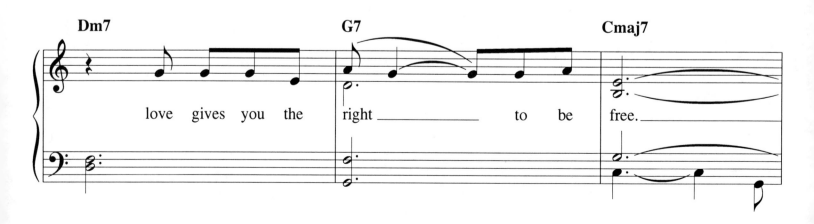

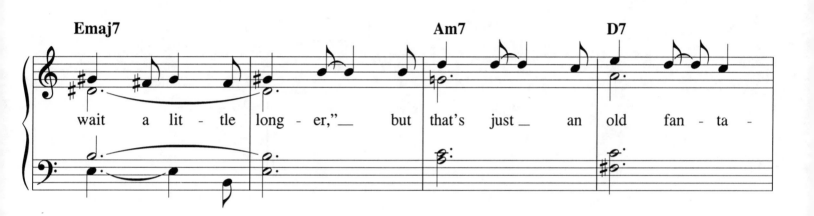

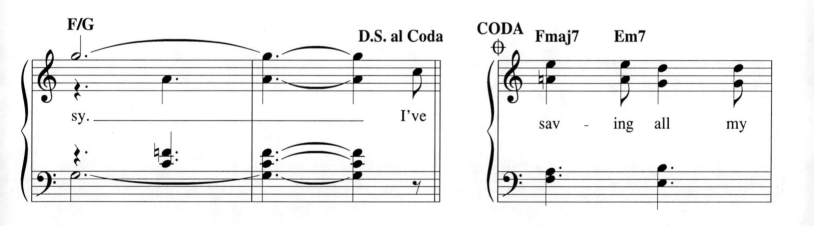

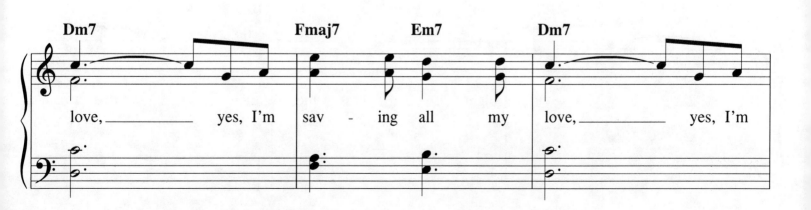

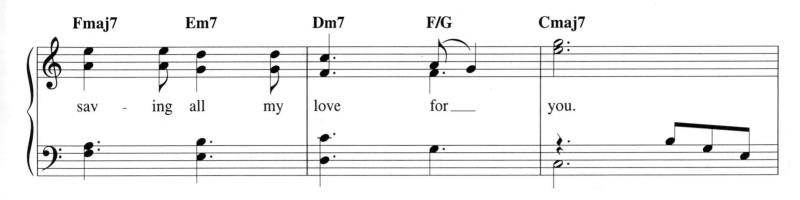

sav - ing all my love for ___ you.

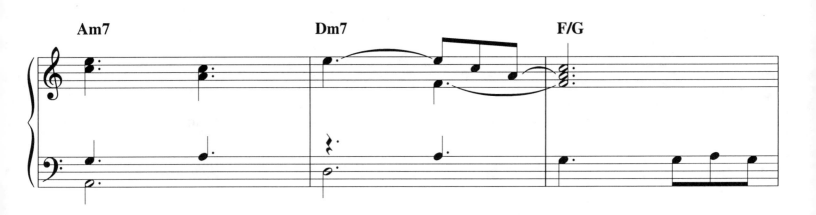

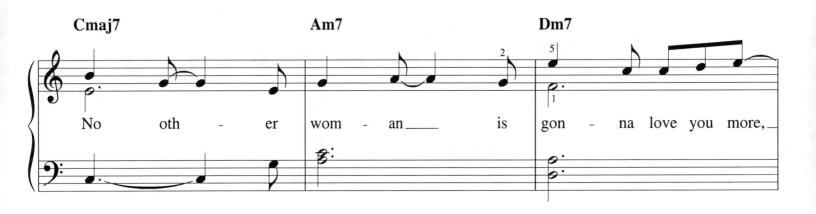

No oth - er wom - an ___ is gon - na love you more,

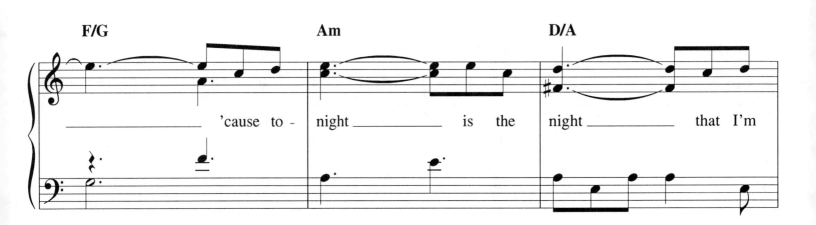

___ 'cause to - night ___ is the night ___ that I'm

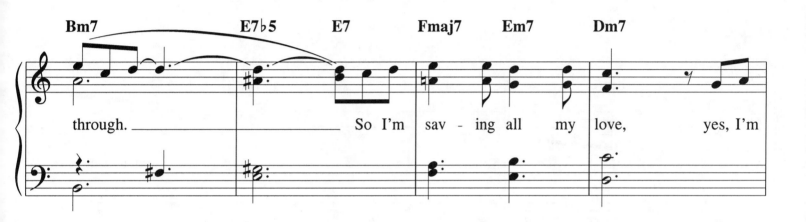

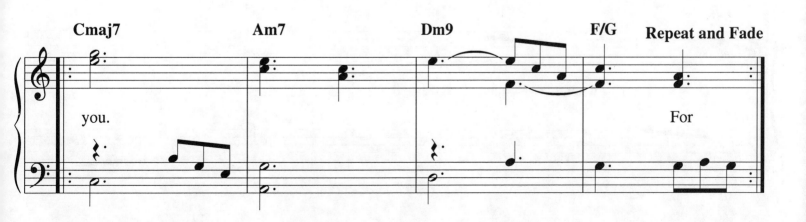

SOMEDAY
from Walt Disney's THE HUNCHBACK OF NOTRE DAME

Music by ALAN MENKEN
Lyrics by STEPHEN SCHWARTZ

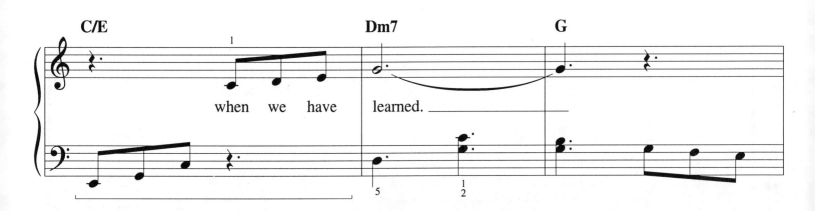

© 1996 Wonderland Music Company, Inc. and Walt Disney Music Company
International Copyright Secured   All Rights Reserved

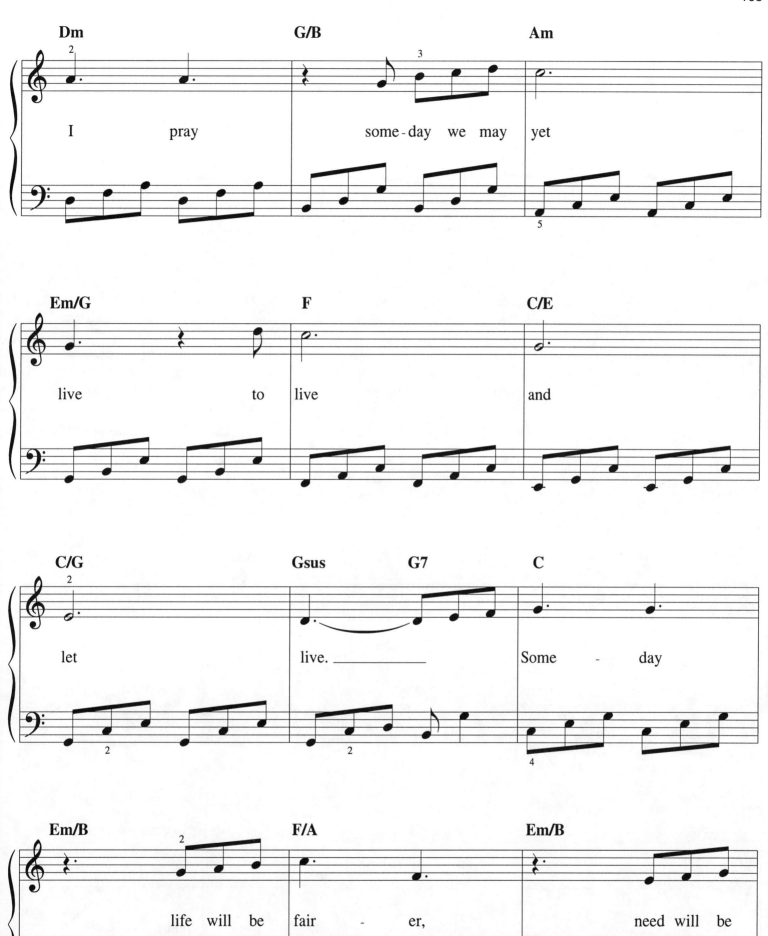

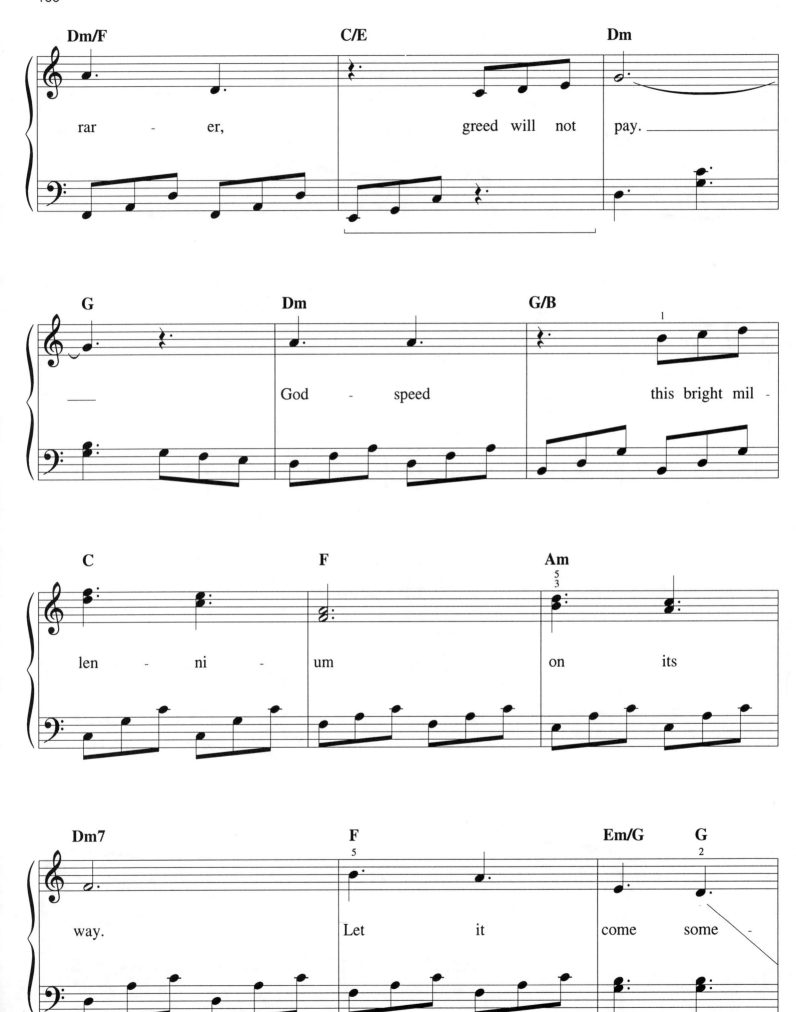

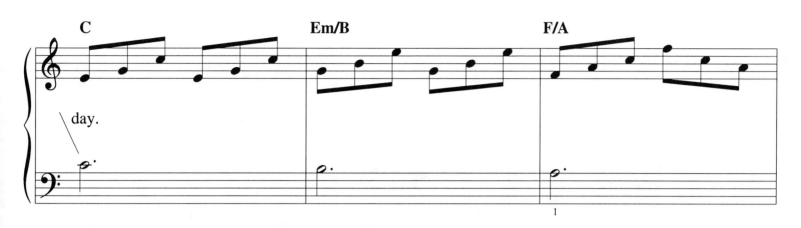

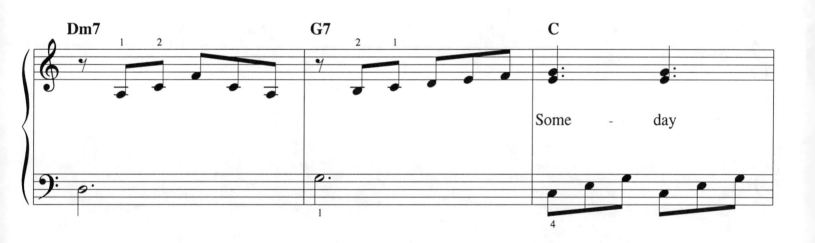

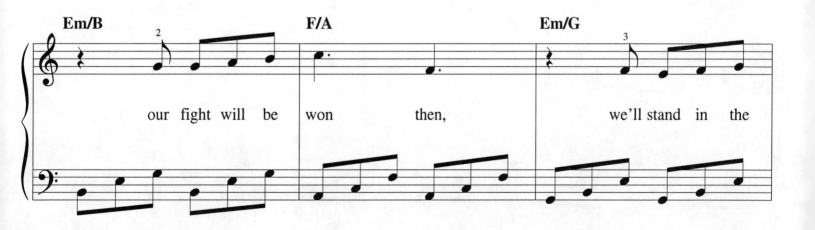

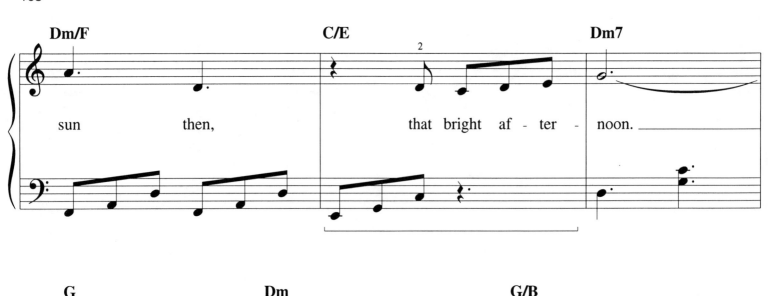

sun   then,   that bright af - ter - noon. _____

_____   Till   then,   on days when the

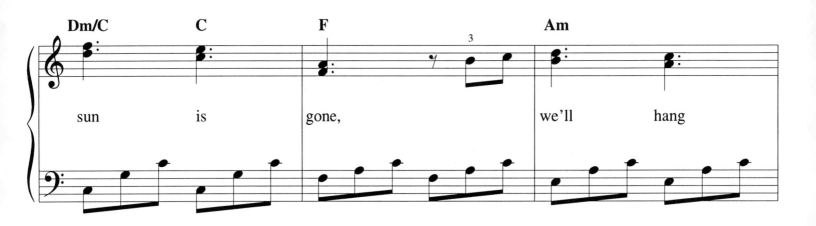

sun   is   gone,   we'll   hang

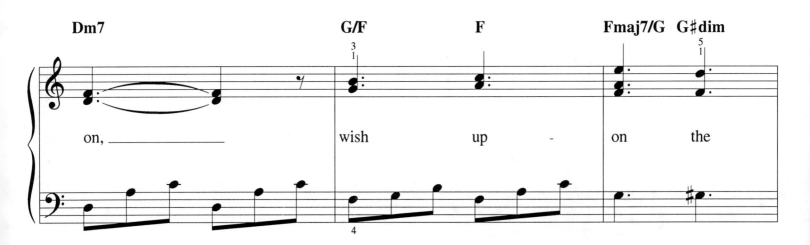

on, _____   wish   up -   on   the

SOMEWHERE OUT THERE
from AN AMERICAN TAIL

Words and Music by JAMES HORNER,
BARRY MANN and CYNTHIA WEIL

Moderately, with expression

© Copyright 1986 by MCA MUSIC PUBLISHING, A Division of UNIVERSAL STUDIOS, INC. and MUSIC CORPORATION OF AMERICA, INC.
International Copyright Secured   All Rights Reserved
MCA music publishing

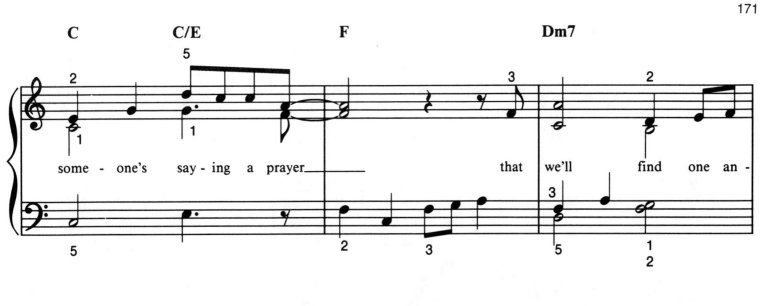

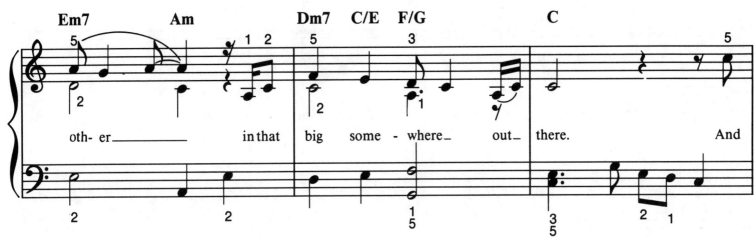

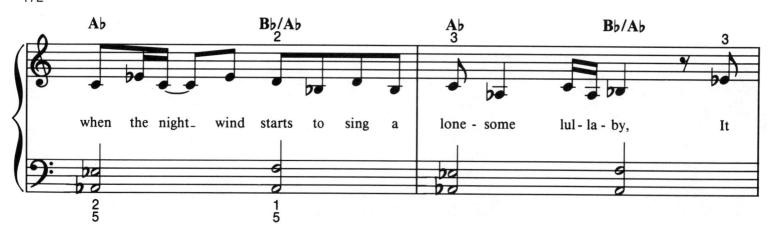

when the night wind starts to sing a lone-some lul-la-by, It

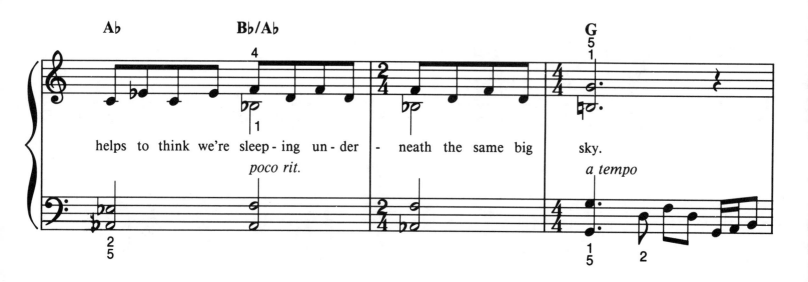

helps to think we're sleep-ing un-der - neath the same big sky. *poco rit.* *a tempo*

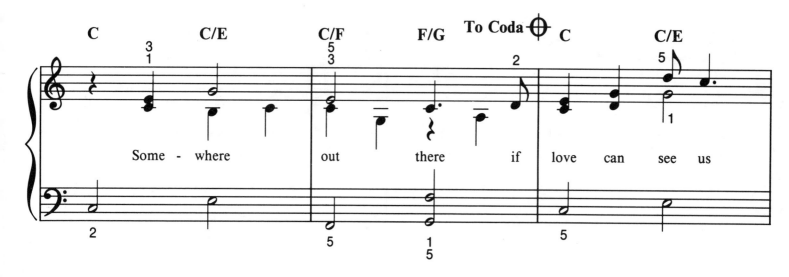

Some - where out there if love can see us

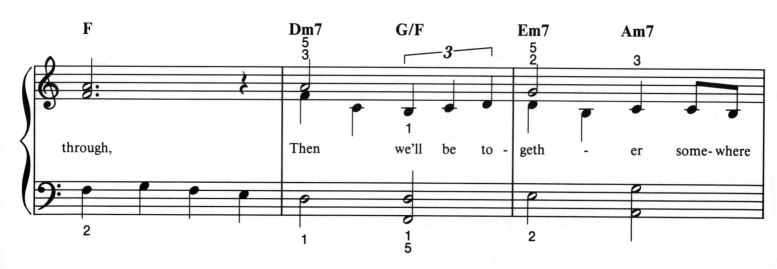

through, Then we'll be to - geth - er some-where

SWEET LOVE

Words and Music by ANITA BAKER,
LOUIS A. JOHNSON and GARY BIAS

Copyright © 1986 Old Brompton Road
Administered by Jobete Music Co., Inc.
All Rights Reserved

I be - lieve ___ I'm in love. ___ Sweet ___ love, ___
I be - lieve ___ in this love. ___
I be - lieve ___ in this love. ___

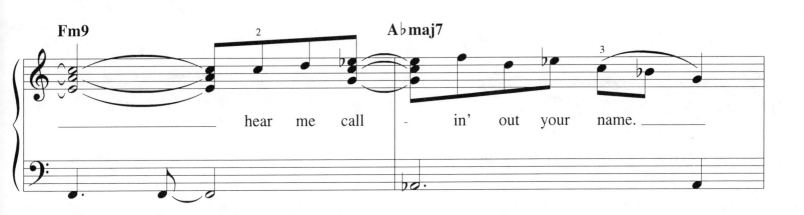

___ hear me call - in' out your name. ___

I feel no shame; ___ I'm in love. ___ Sweet ___ love,

___ don't you ev - er go a - way. ___ It - 'll

176

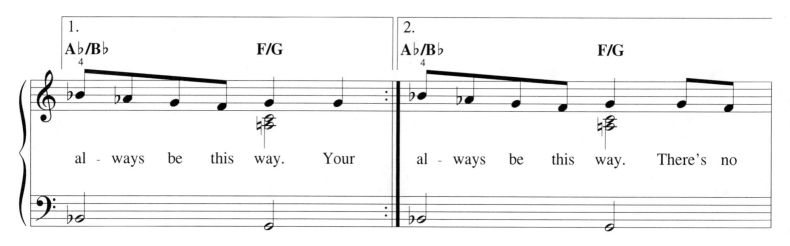

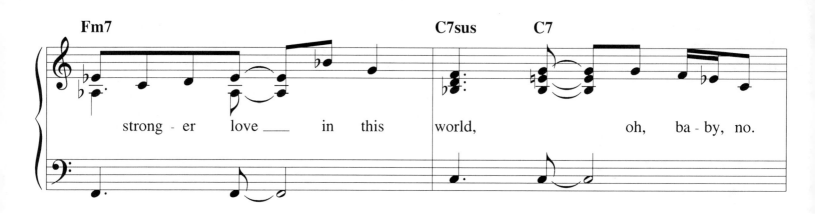

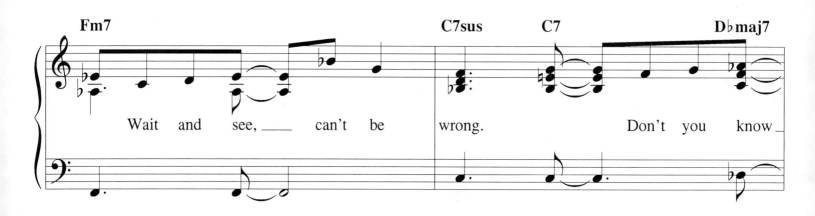

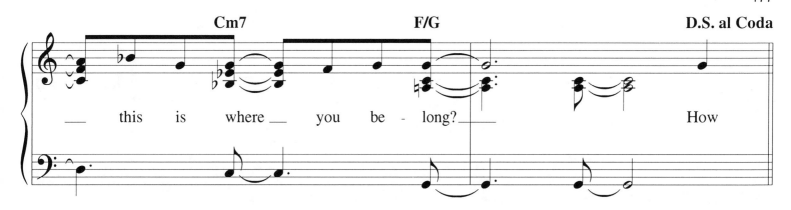

this is where ___ you be - long? ___ How

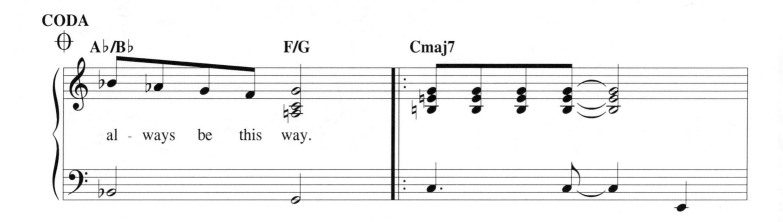

al - ways be this way.

THE SWEETEST DAYS

Words and Music by JON LIND,
PHIL GALDSTON and WENDY WALDMAN

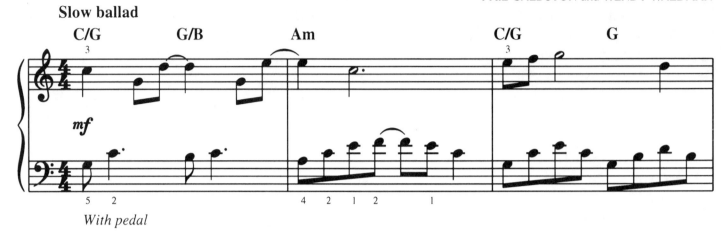

With pedal

You and I _____ in this   mo - ment,
There are   times _____ that   scare __ me.   We'll

hold-ing the night _ so _ close,_   hang-ing on,_____ still un-bro-
rat - tle the house_ like the   wind,_   both of us_____ so un-bend-

- ken _   while out-side the thun - der _ rolls._____
- ing. _   We bat - tle the fear _ with - in._____

© 1994 EMI VIRGIN SONGS, INC., BIG MYSTIQUE MUSIC, FAMOUS MUSIC CORPORATION, KAZZOOM MUSIC, INC.,
WINDSWEPT PACIFIC ENTERTAINMENT CO. d/b/a LONGITUDE MUSIC CO. and MOON AND STARS MUSIC
All Rights for BIG MYSTIQUE MUSIC Controlled and Administered by EMI VIRGIN SONGS, INC.
All Rights for KAZZOOM MUSIC, INC. Controlled and Administered by FAMOUS MUSIC CORPORATION
All Rights Reserved   International Copyright Secured   Used by Permission

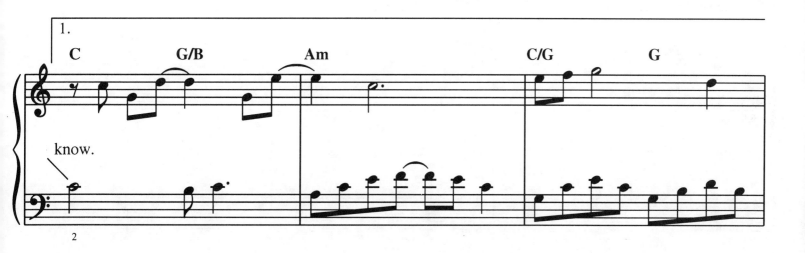

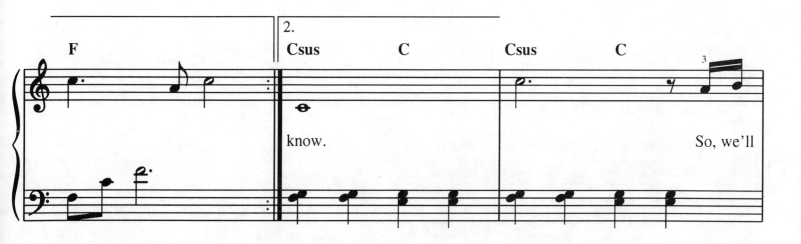

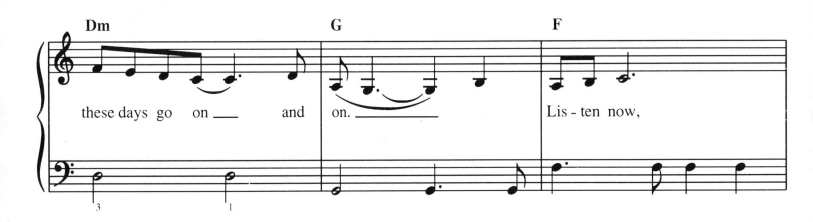

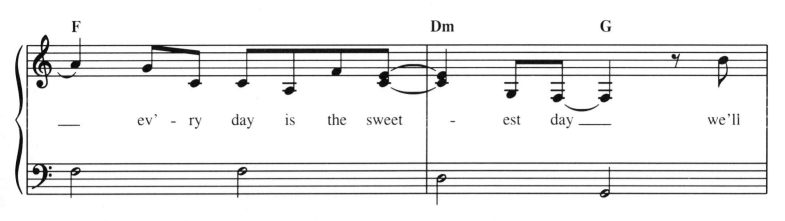

ev' - ry day is the sweet - est day _____ we'll

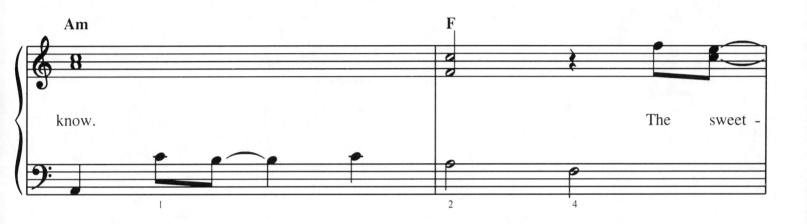

know. The sweet -

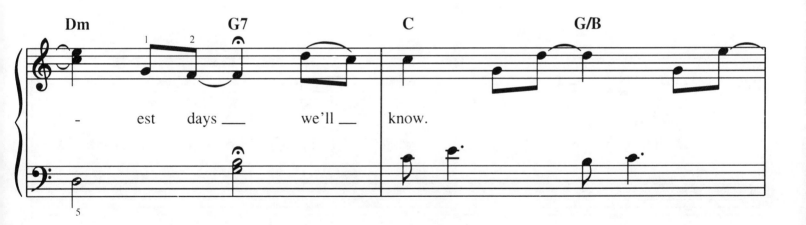

- est days _____ we'll ___ know.

rit.

Ped. _____

THAT'S WHAT LOVE IS FOR

Words and Music by MARK MUELLER,
MICHAEL OMARTIAN and AMY GRANT

Moderate Ballad

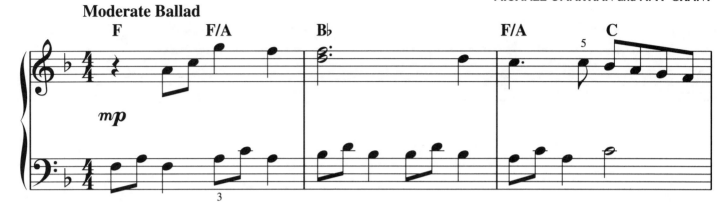

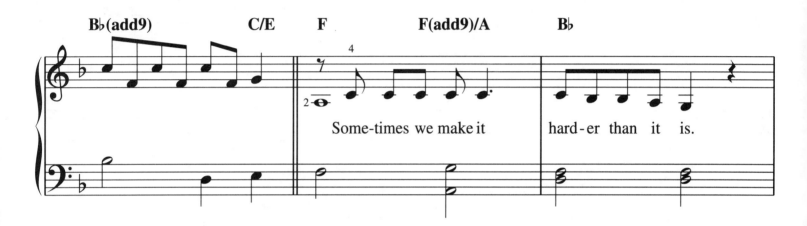

Some-times we make it hard-er than it is.

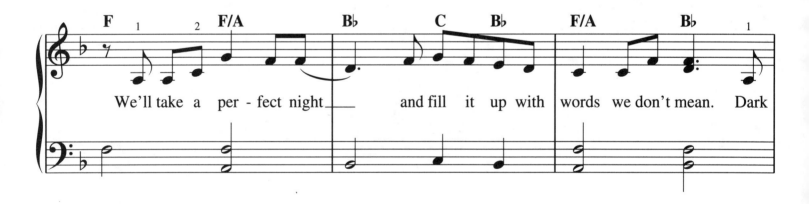

We'll take a per-fect night___ and fill it up with words we don't mean. Dark

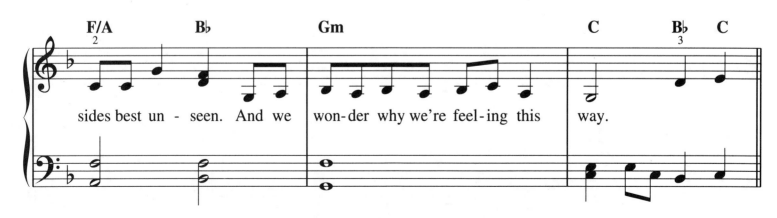

sides best un - seen. And we won-der why we're feel-ing this way.

© Copyright 1991 by MCA MUSIC PUBLISHING, A Division of UNIVERSAL STUDIOS, INC., MOO MAISON, ALL NATIONS MUSIC and AGE TO AGE MUSIC, INC.
All Rights for MOO MAISON Controlled and Administered by MCA MUSIC PUBLISHING, A Division of UNIVERSAL STUDIOS, INC.
All Rights for AGE TO AGE MUSIC, INC. Administered by BH PUBLISHING
International Copyright Secured   All Rights Reserved

MCA music publishing

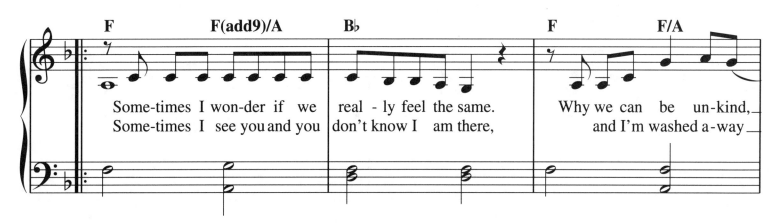

Some-times I won-der if we real - ly feel the same. Why we can be un-kind,
Some-times I see you and you don't know I am there, and I'm washed a-way

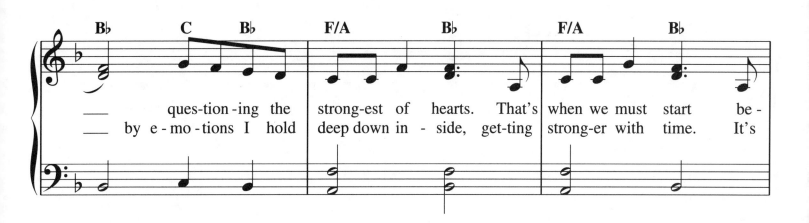

___ ques-tion -ing the strong-est of hearts. That's when we must start be -
___ by e - mo -tions I hold deep down in - side, get-ting strong-er with time. It's

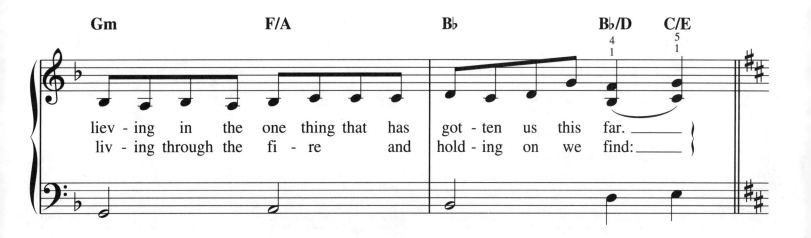

liev - ing in the one thing that has got - ten us this far. _____
liv - ing through the fi – re and hold - ing on we find: _____

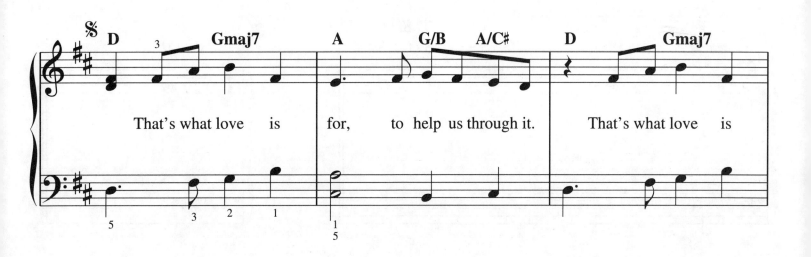

That's what love is for, to help us through it. That's what love is

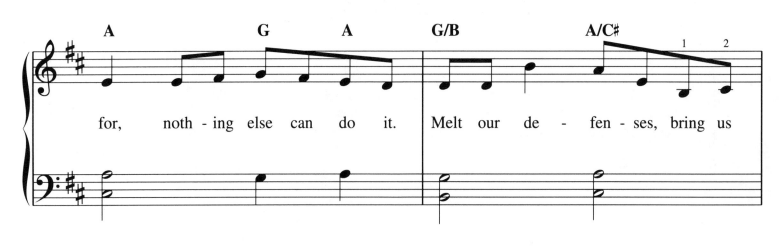

for, noth - ing else can do it. Melt our de - fen - ses, bring us

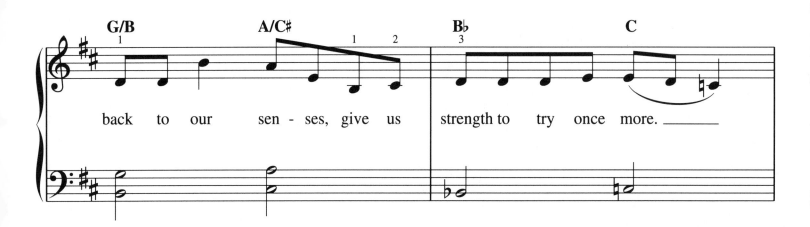

back to our sen - ses, give us strength to try once more. _____

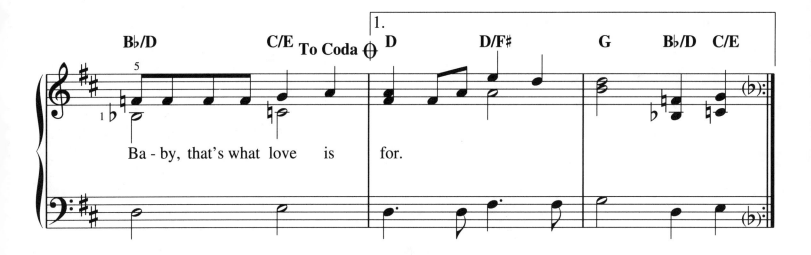

Ba - by, that's what love is for.

for.

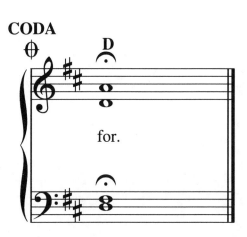

for.

THROUGH THE YEARS

Words and Music by STEVE DORFF
and MARTY PANZER

With tenderness

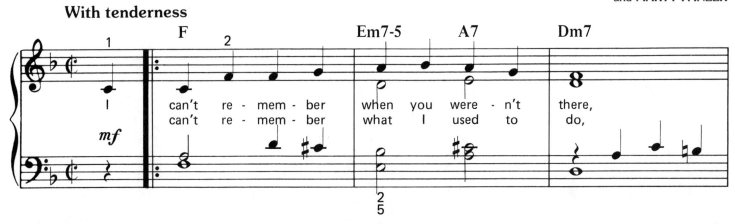

I
can't re-mem-ber when you were-n't there,
can't re-mem-ber what I used to do,

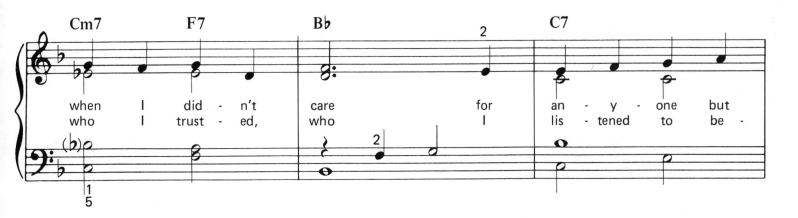

when I did-n't care
who I trust-ed, who I
for
lis-tened to be-

an-y-one but

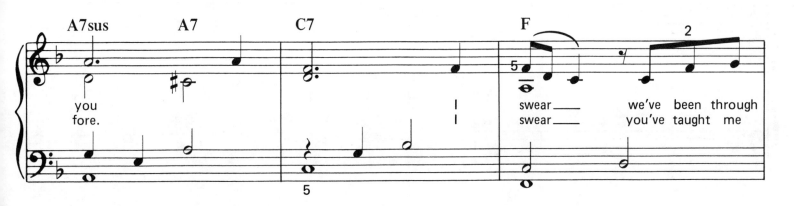

you
fore.
I
I
swear____ we've been through
swear____ you've taught me

ev-'ry-thing there is.
ev-'ry-thing I know.
Can't i-mag-ine
Can't i-mag-ine
an-y-thing we've
need-ing some-one

Copyright © 1980 by Careers-BMG Music Publishing, Inc. and SwaneeBRAVO! Music
International Copyright Secured All Rights Reserved

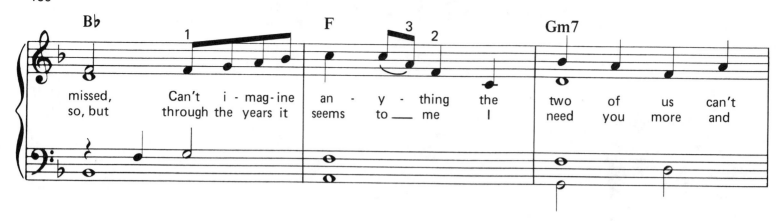

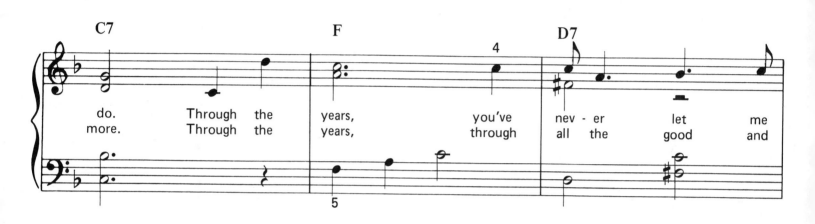

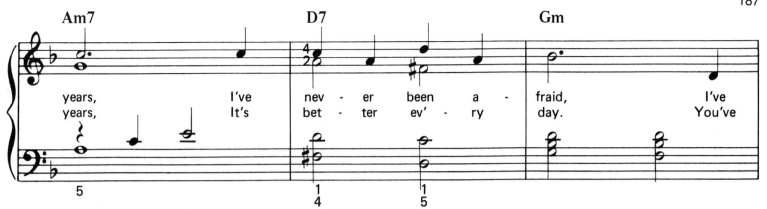

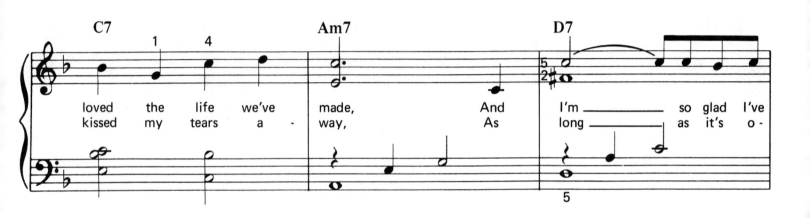

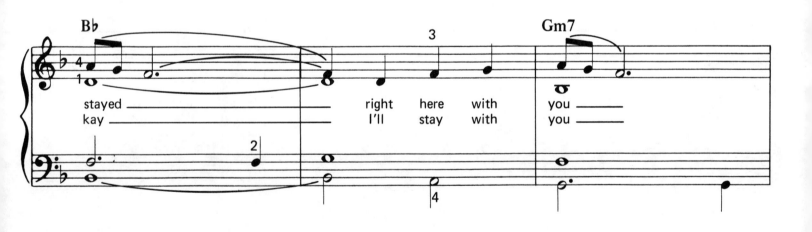

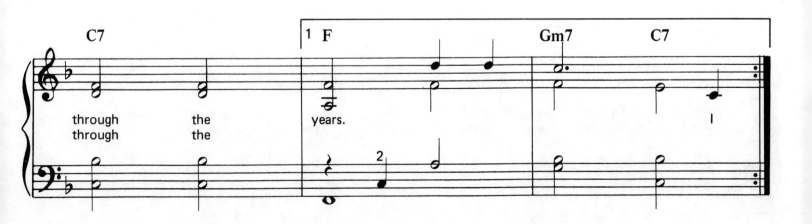

188

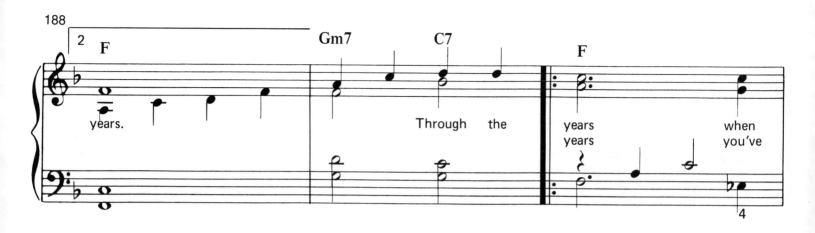

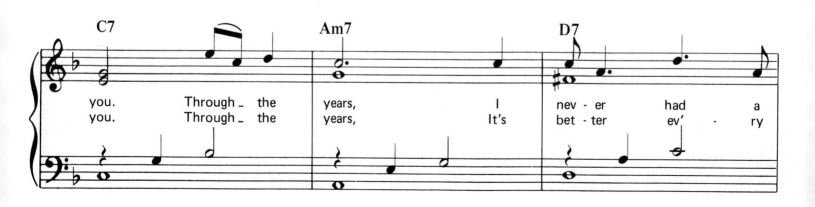

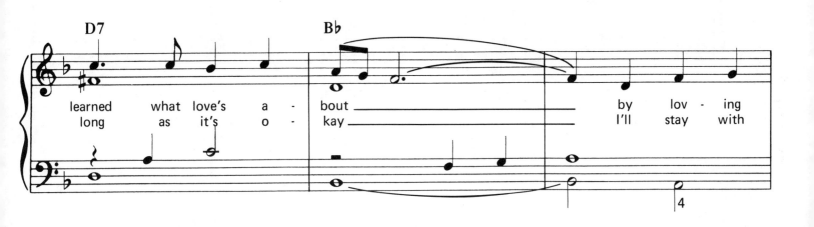

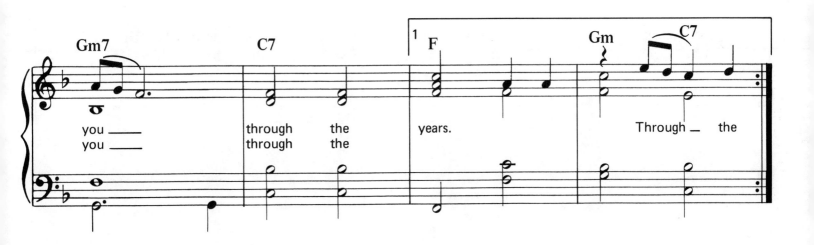

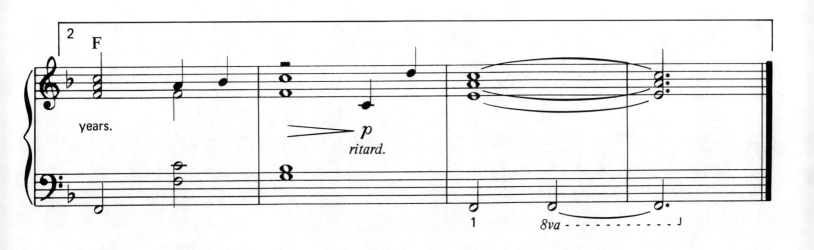

THAT'S WHAT LOVE IS ALL ABOUT

Words and Music by MICHAEL BOLTON
and ERIC KAZ

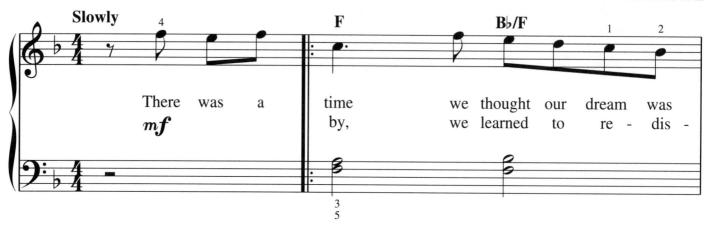

There was a time, we thought our dream was
mf

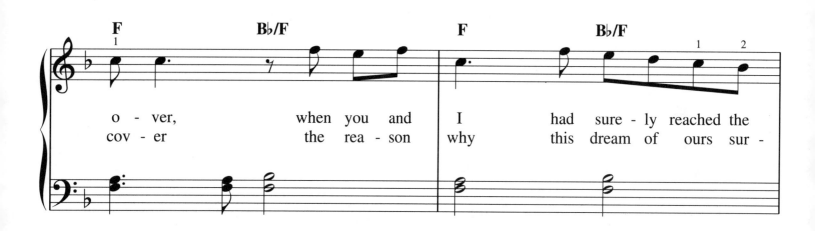

o - ver, when you and I had sure - ly reached the
cov - er the rea - son why this dream of ours sur -

end. Still, here we are. The flame is strong as
vives. Through thick and thin, we're des - tined for each

© 1987 EMI APRIL MUSIC INC., IS HOT MUSIC and KAZ MUSIC CO.
All Rights Controlled and Administered by EMI APRIL MUSIC INC.
All Rights Reserved   International Copyright Secured   Used by Permission

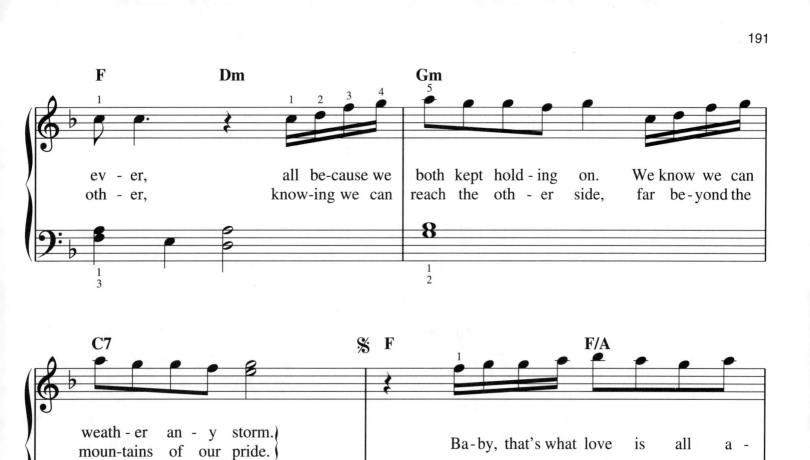

ev - er,   all be-cause we | both kept hold - ing   on.   We know we can
oth - er,   know-ing we can | reach the oth - er side,   far be - yond the

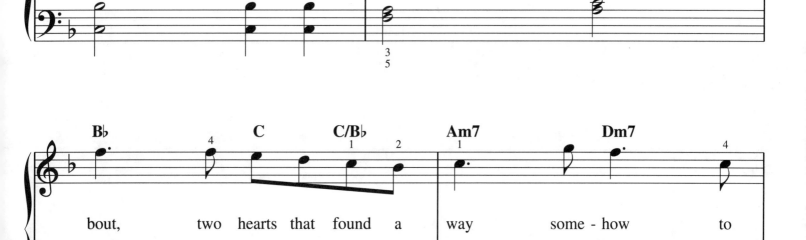

weath - er an - y storm. | Ba-by, that's what love   is   all   a -
moun-tains of our pride. |

bout,   two hearts that found a | way   some - how   to

keep the fi - re burn - ing. | Some-thing we could nev - er live with -

192

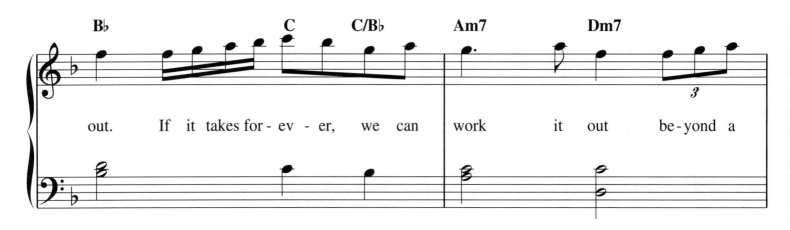

out.   If it takes for - ev - er,   we can | work   it   out   be - yond a

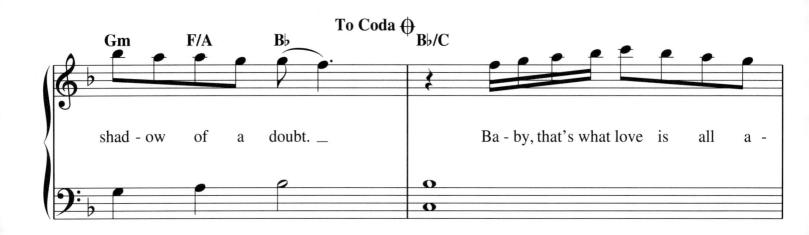

shad - ow   of   a   doubt. __ | Ba - by, that's what love is   all   a -

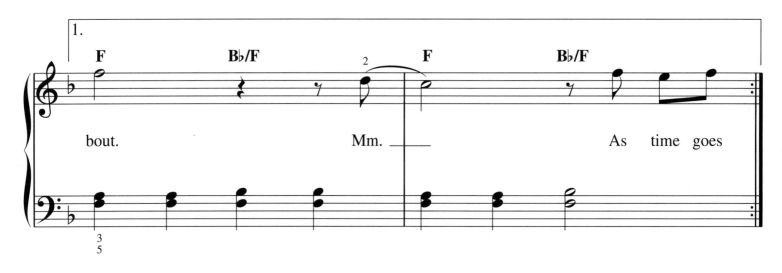

1.
bout.   Mm. __   As   time goes

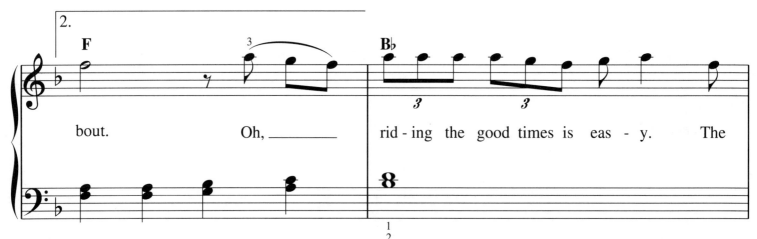

2.
bout.   Oh, _____   rid - ing the good times is eas - y.   The

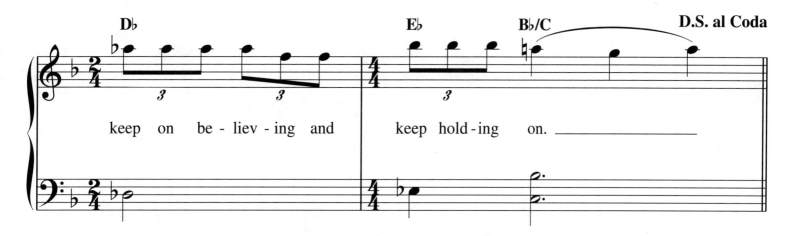

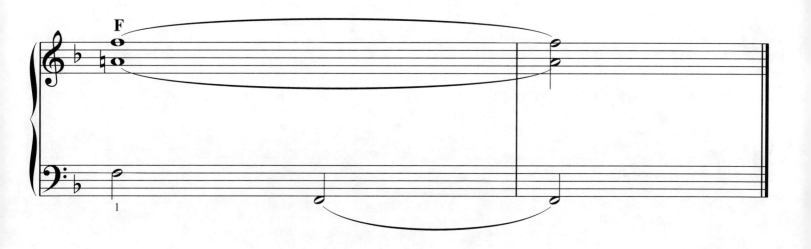

TONIGHT I CELEBRATE MY LOVE

Words and Music by MICHAEL MASSER
and GERRY GOFFIN

© 1983 SCREEN GEMS-EMI MUSIC INC., LAUREN-WESLEY MUSIC and ALMO MUSIC CORP.
All Rights for LAUREN-WESLEY MUSIC Controlled and Administered by SCREEN GEMS-EMI MUSIC INC.
All Rights Reserved   International Copyright Secured   Used by Permission

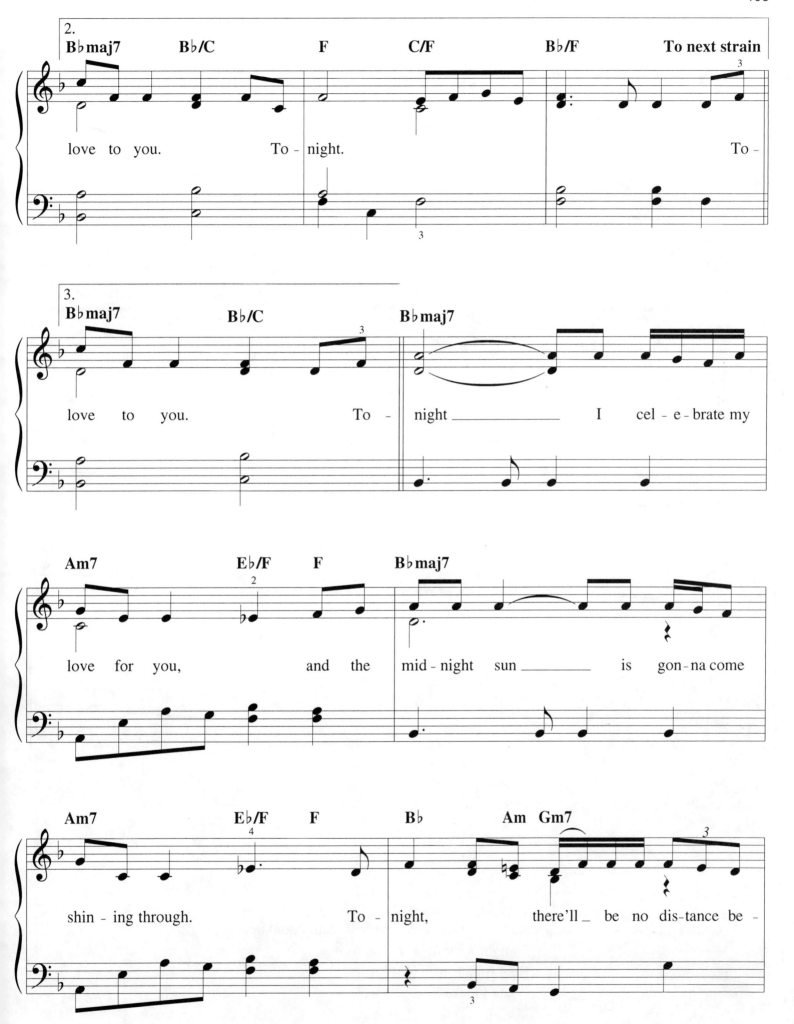

196

Additional Lyrics

3.   Tonight I celebrate my love for you
     And soon this old world will seem brand new.
     Tonight we will both discover
     How friends turn into lovers,
     When I make love to you.

A WHOLE NEW WORLD
(Aladdin's Theme)
from Walt Disney's ALADDIN

Music by ALAN MENKEN
Lyrics by TIM RICE

Slowly and sweetly

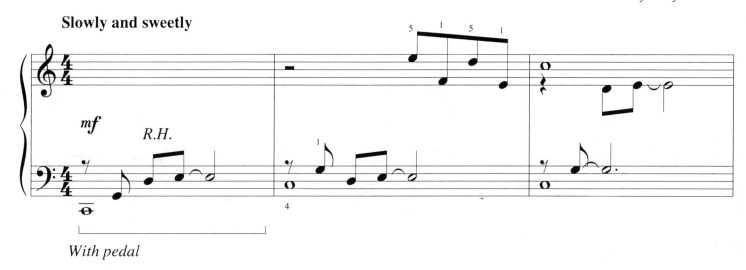

With pedal

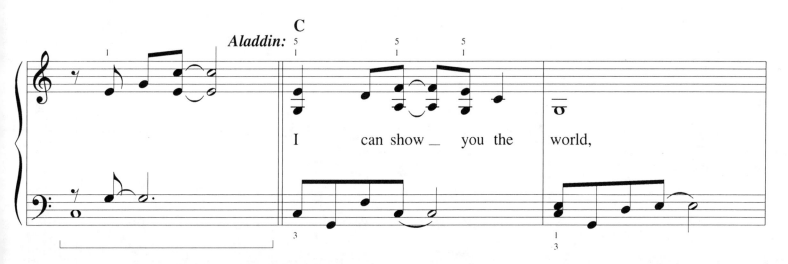

I can show ___ you the world,

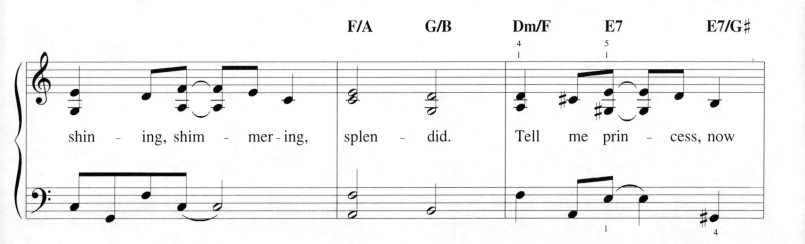

shin - ing, shim - mer - ing, splen - did. Tell me prin - cess, now

© 1992 Wonderland Music Company, Inc. and Walt Disney Music Company
International Copyright Secured   All Rights Reserved

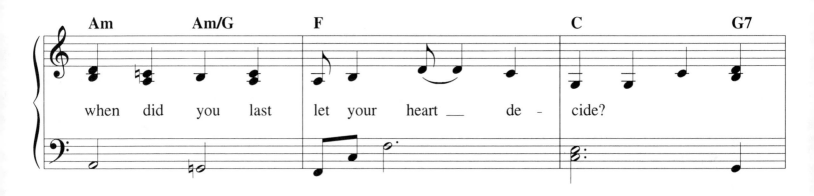

when did you last let your heart ___ de - cide?

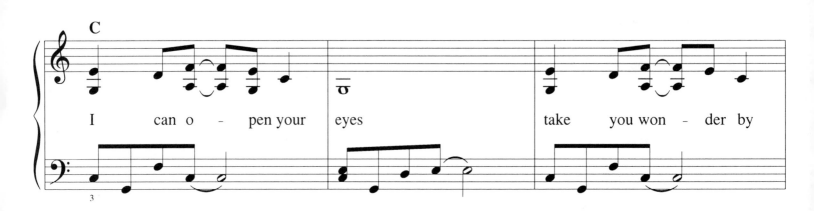

I can o - pen your eyes take you won - der by

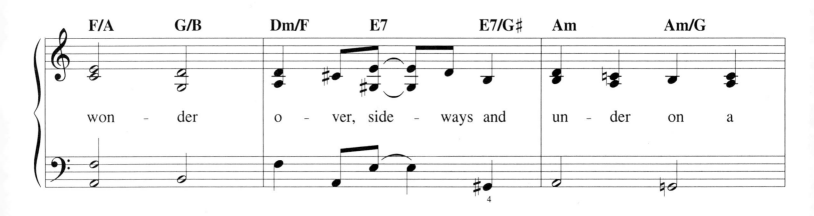

won - der o - ver, side - ways and un - der on a

mag-ic car - pet ride. A whole new world

199

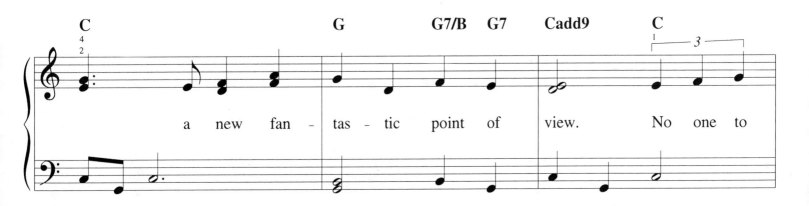

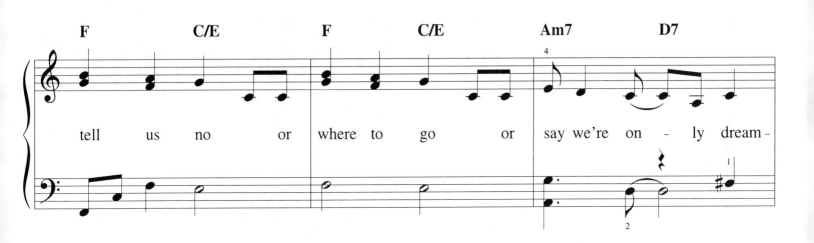

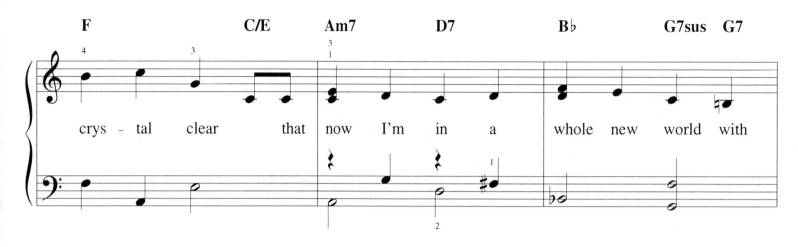

crys - tal   clear   that   now I'm   in   a   whole   new   world   with

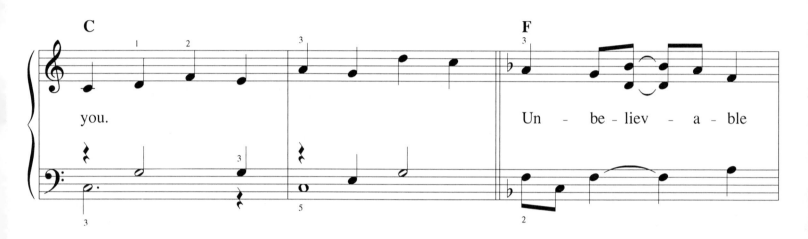

you.   Un - be - liev - a - ble

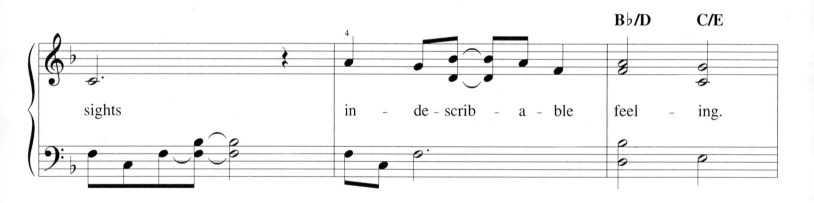

sights   in - de - scrib - a - ble   feel - ing.

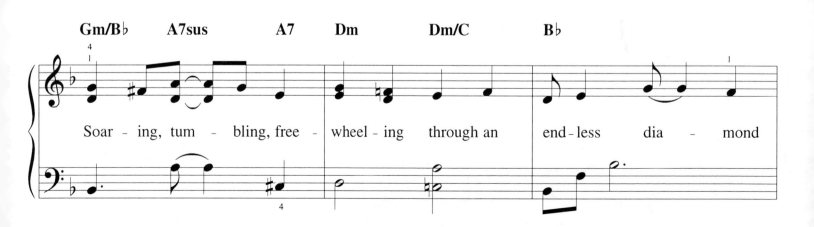

Soar - ing, tum - bling, free - wheel - ing   through an   end - less   dia - mond

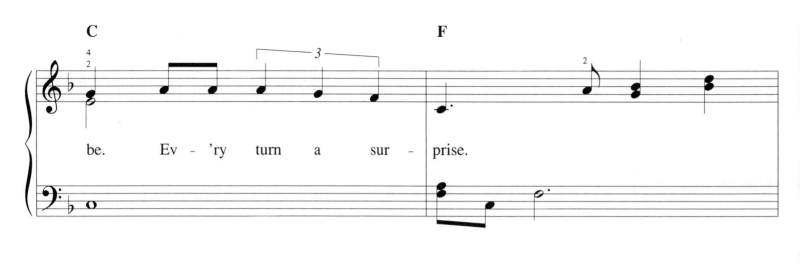

be. Ev - 'ry turn a sur - prise.

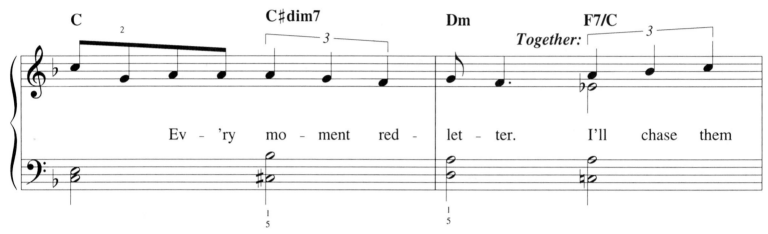

Ev - 'ry mo - ment red - let - ter. I'll chase them

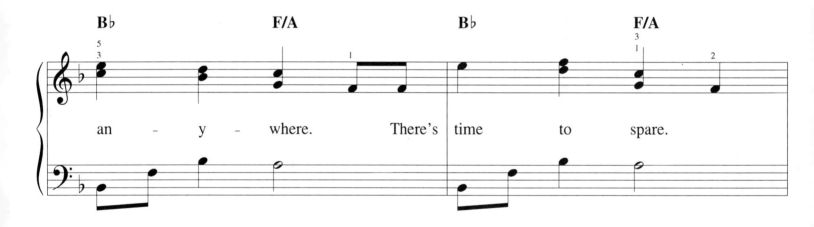

an - y - where. There's time to spare.

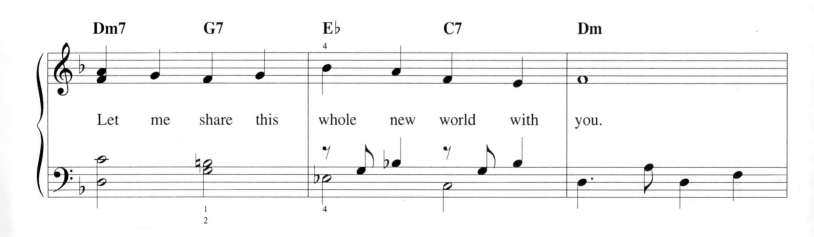

Let me share this whole new world with you.

UNCHAINED MELODY

Lyric by HY ZARET
Music by ALEX NORTH

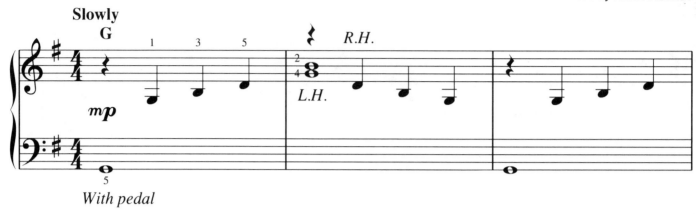

Oh, my love, my

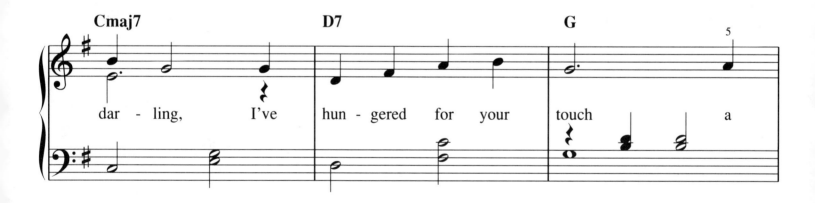

dar - ling, I've hun - gered for your touch a

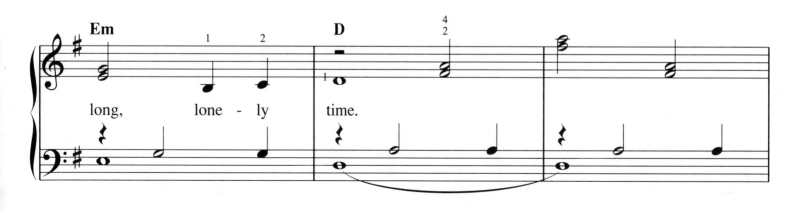

long, lone - ly time.

© 1955 (Renewed) FRANK MUSIC CORP.
All Rights Reserved

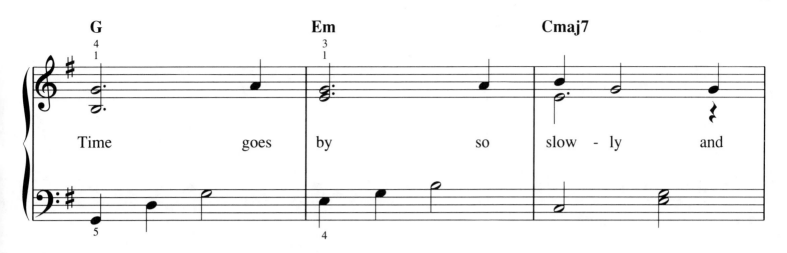

G   Em   Cmaj7

Time   goes   by   so   slow - ly   and

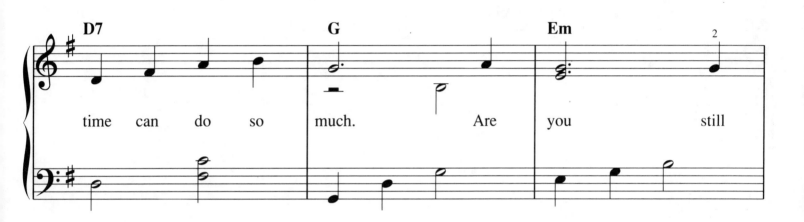

D7   G   Em

time   can   do   so   much.   Are   you   still

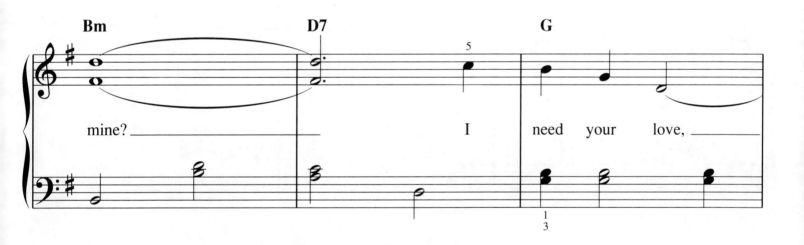

Bm   D7   G

mine? _____   I   need   your   love, _____

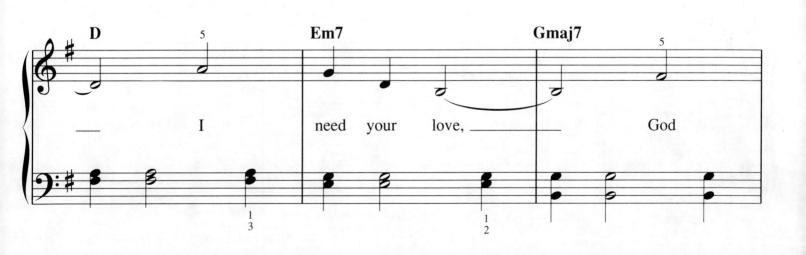

D   Em7   Gmaj7

__   I   need   your   love, _____   God

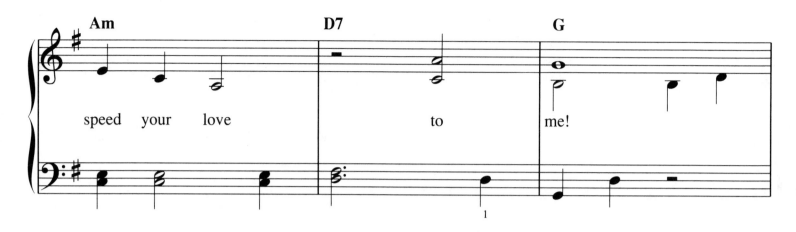

speed   your   love   to   me!

Slightly faster

To Coda ⊕ C   D

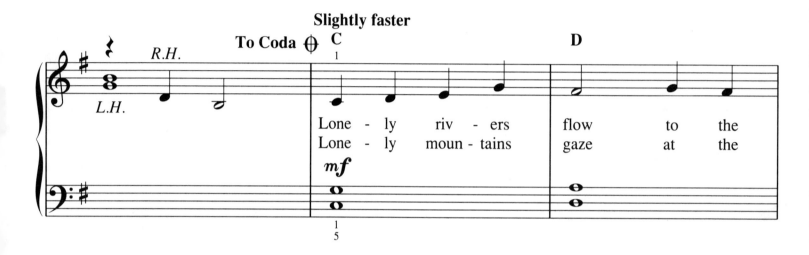

Lone - ly   riv - ers   flow   to   the
Lone - ly   moun - tains   gaze   at   the

C   D   C

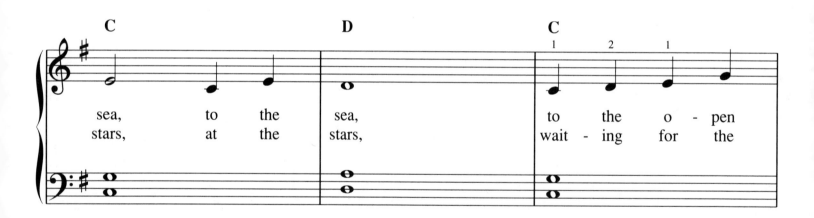

sea,   to   the   sea,   to   the   o - pen
stars,   at   the   stars,   wait - ing   for   the

D   G

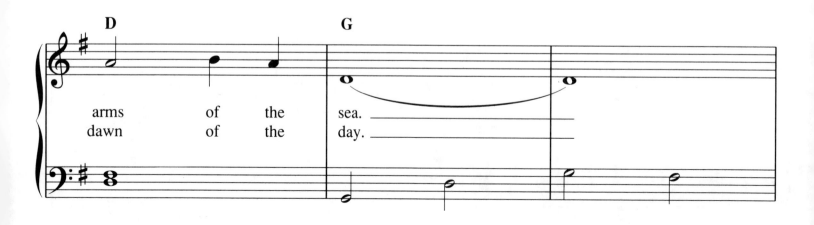

arms   of   the   sea. _____
dawn   of   the   day. _____

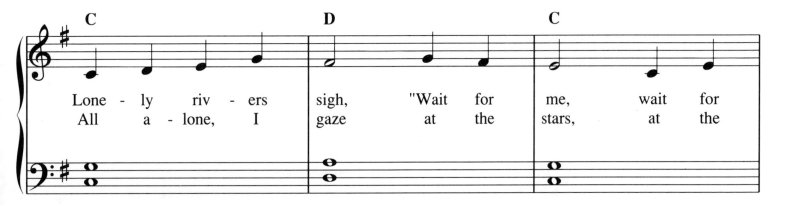

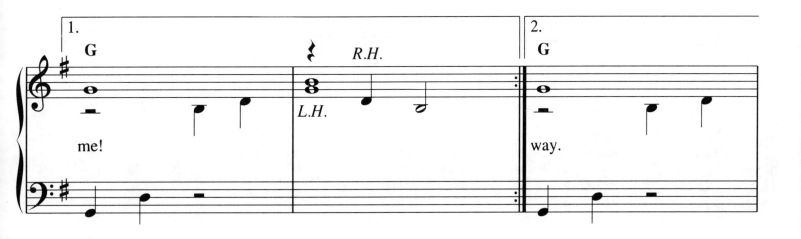

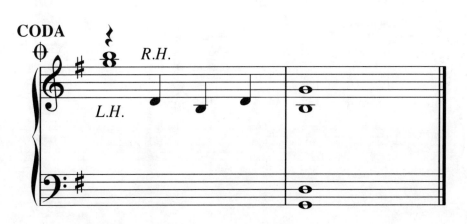

UP WHERE WE BELONG

from the Paramount Picture AN OFFICER AND A GENTLEMAN

Words by WILL JENNINGS
Music by BUFFY SAINTE-MARIE and JACK NITZSCHE

Copyright © 1982 by Famous Music Corporation and Ensign Music Corporation
International Copyright Secured   All Rights Reserved

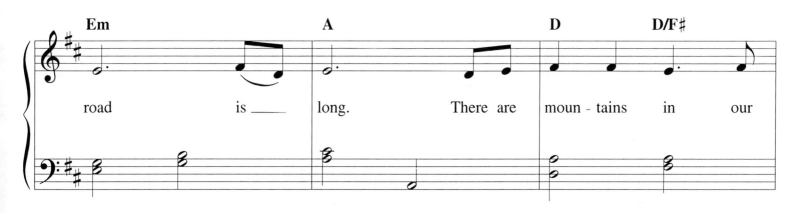

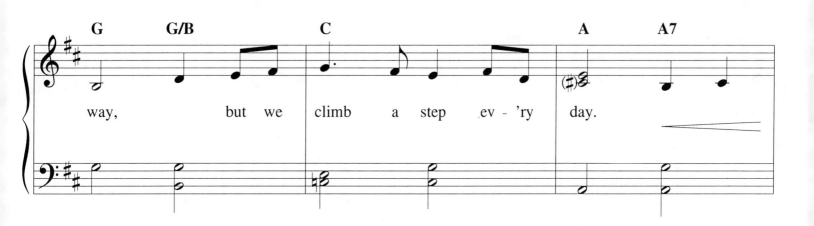

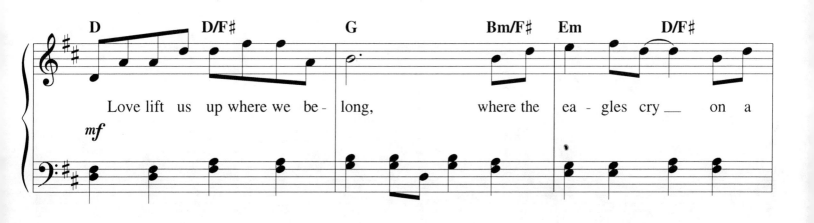

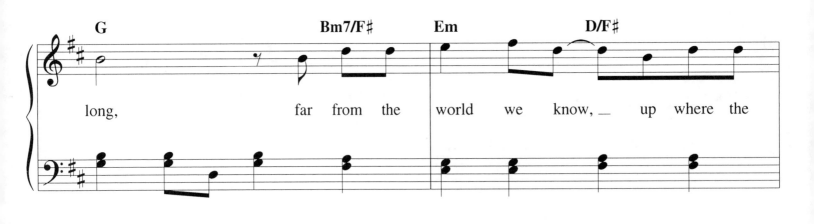

long,   far from the   world   we   know, __   up   where the

clear   winds   blow. __

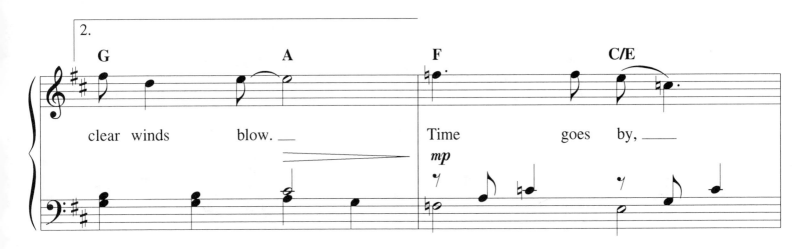

clear   winds   blow. __   Time   goes   by, ____   a -

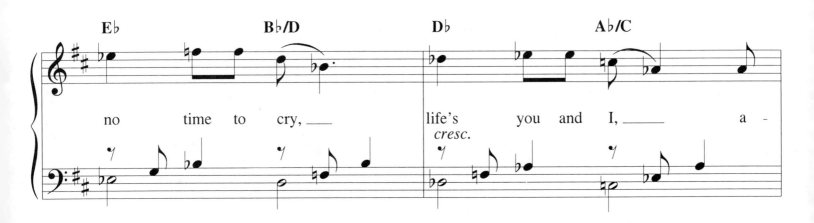

no   time   to   cry, ___   life's   you   and   I, ____   a -

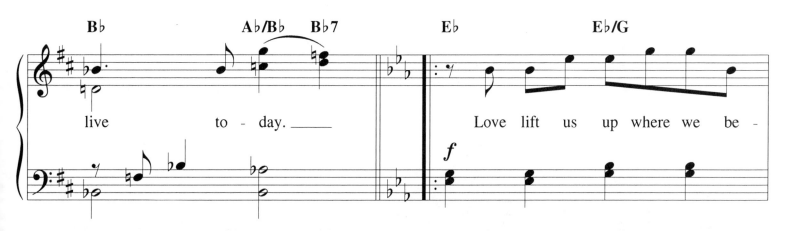

live to - day. _____ Love lift us up where we be -

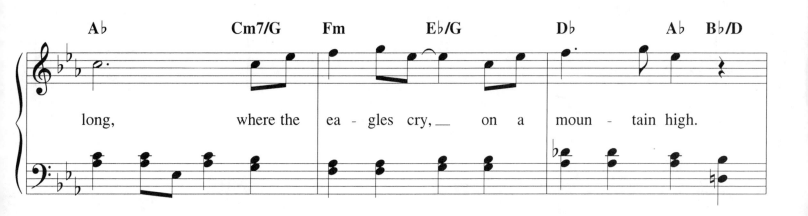

long, where the ea - gles cry, _ on a moun - tain high.

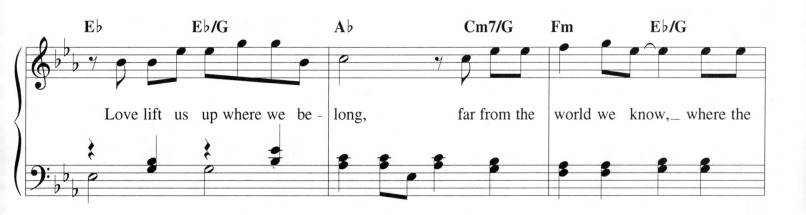

Love lift us up where we be - long, far from the world we know, _ where the

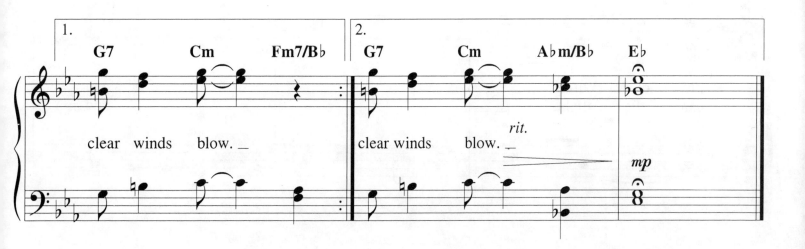

1.
clear winds blow. _

2.
clear winds blow. _

WE'RE IN THIS LOVE TOGETHER

Words and Music by ROGER MURRAH
and KEITH STEGALL

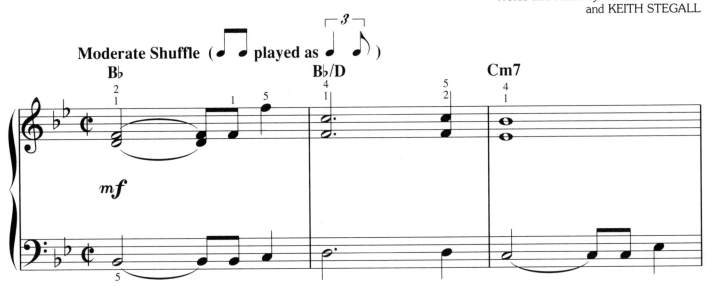

It's like a dia-mond ring it's a
It's like a rain - y night and ___

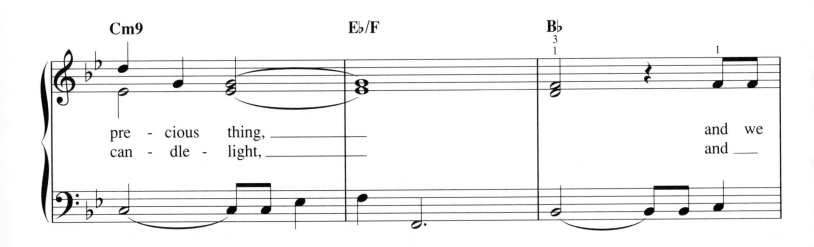

pre - cious thing, ___
can - dle - light, ___

and we
and ___

© 1980 EMI BLACKWOOD MUSIC INC. and MAGIC CASTLE MUSIC, INC.
All Rights Controlled and Administered by EMI BLACKWOOD MUSIC INC.
All Rights Reserved   International Copyright Secured   Used by Permission

214

sweet - er all___ the time.___

Don't you know

WHEN YOU SAY NOTHING AT ALL

Words and Music by DON SCHLITZ
and PAUL OVERSTREET

Moderately Slow

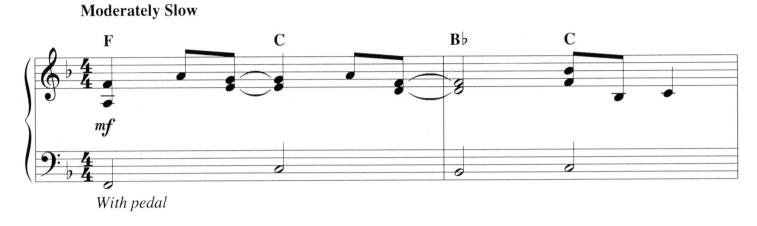

mf

With pedal

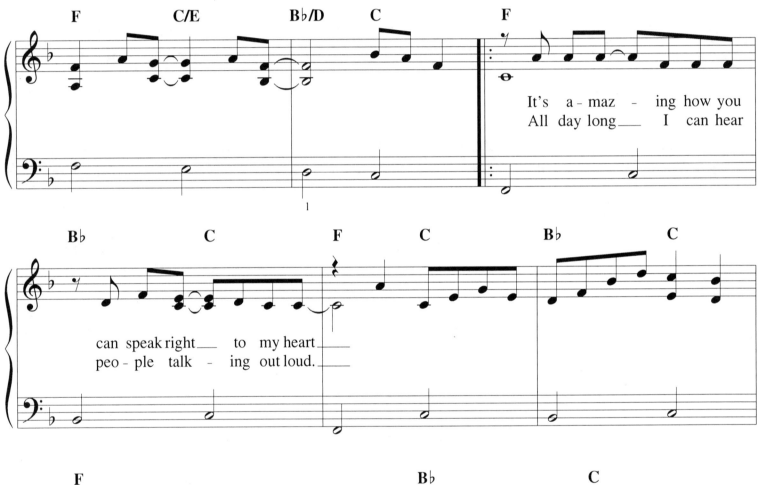

It's a - maz - ing how you
All day long___ I can hear

can speak right___ to my heart___
peo - ple talk - ing out loud.

With - out say - ing a word___ you can light up the dark.
But when you___ hold me near___ you drown out the crowd.

© Copyright 1988 by MCA MUSIC PUBLISHING, A Division of UNIVERSAL STUDIOS, INC., DON SCHLITZ MUSIC, SCREEN GEMS-EMI MUSIC INC. and SCARLET MOON MUSIC
All Rights for DON SCHLITZ MUSIC Controlled and Administered by MCA MUSIC PUBLISHING, A Division of UNIVERSAL STUDIOS, INC.
All Rights for SCARLET MOON MUSIC Administered by COPYRIGHT MANAGEMENT, INC., Nashville, TN
International Copyright Secured   All Rights Reserved
MCA music publishing

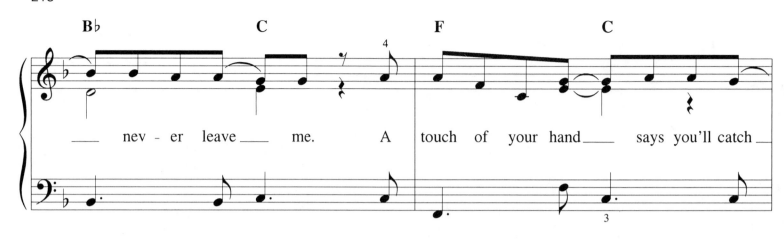

nev - er leave ___ me.   A   touch of your hand___ says you'll catch

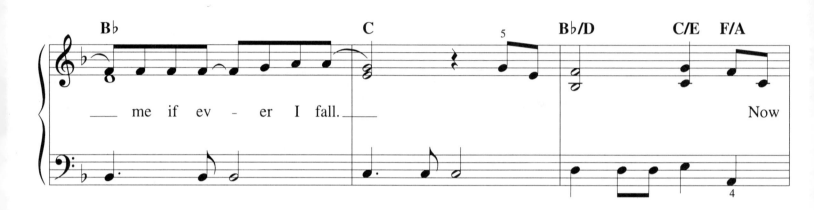

___ me if ev - er I fall.___   Now

you say it best___   when you say noth-ing at all.___

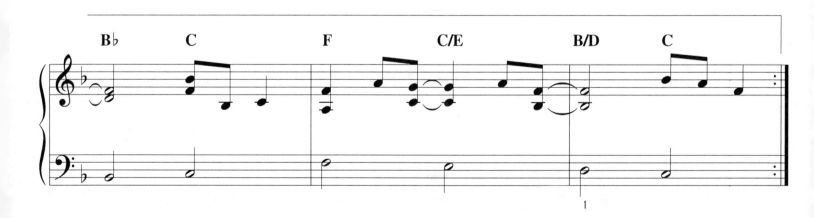

when you say noth-ing at all.___

D.S. al Coda

The

CODA

when you say noth-ing at all.___

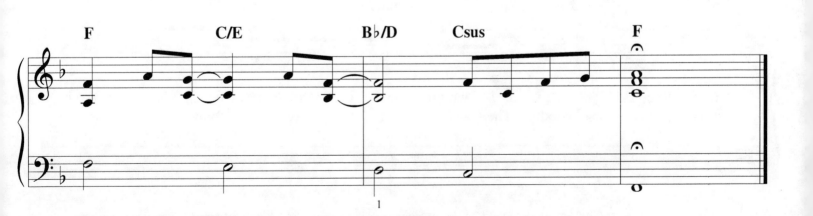

YOU MEAN THE WORLD TO ME

Words and Music by BABYFACE,
L.A. REID and DARYL SIMMONS

Copyright © 1993 Sony ATV/Songs LLC, ECAF Music, Warner-Tamerlane Publishing Corp., Stiff Shirt Music and Boobie-Loo Music
All Rights on behalf of Sony/ATV Songs LLC and ECAF Music Administered by Sony/ATV Music Publishing, 8 Music Square West, Nashville, TN 37203
All Rights on behalf of Stiff Shirt Music and Boobie-Loo Music Administered by Warner-Tamerlane Publishing Corp.
International Copyright Secured   All Rights Reserved

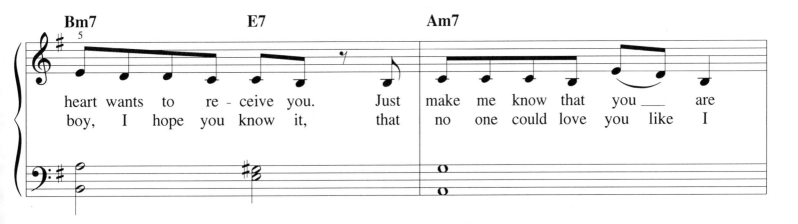

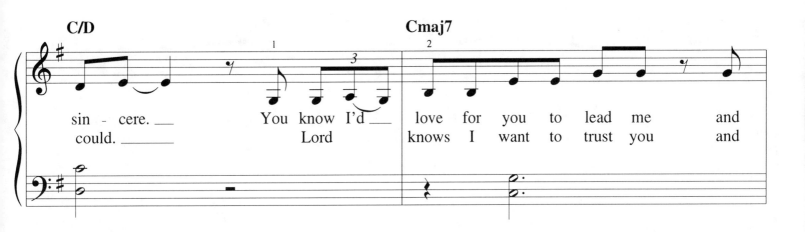

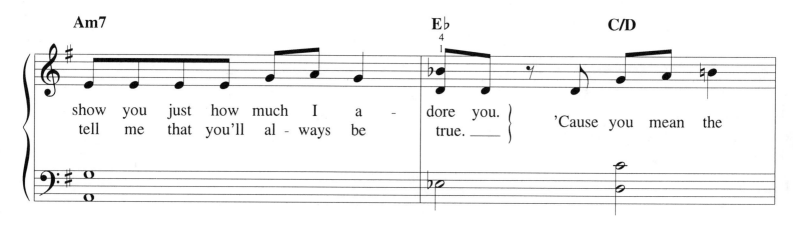

Am7 ... **Eb** ... **C/D**

show you just how much I a - dore you. 'Cause you mean the
tell me that you'll al - ways be true. ___

G ... **G/F** ... **C/E**

world to me, you are my ev - 'ry-thing, I swear the on - ly thing that mat-ters,

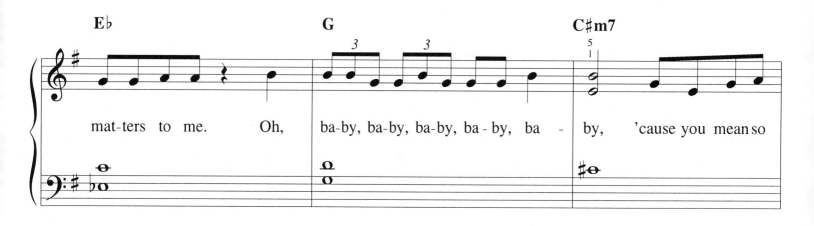

Eb ... **G** ... **C♯m7**

mat-ters to me. Oh, ba-by, ba-by, ba-by, ba-by, ba - by, 'cause you mean so

Am7 ... 1. **Eb** **C/D** ... 2. **Eb** **C/D**

much to ___ me. Now it's There's a

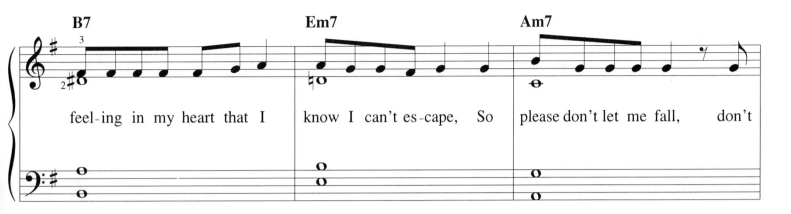

224

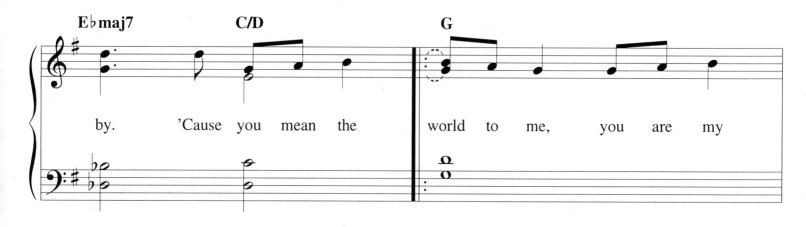

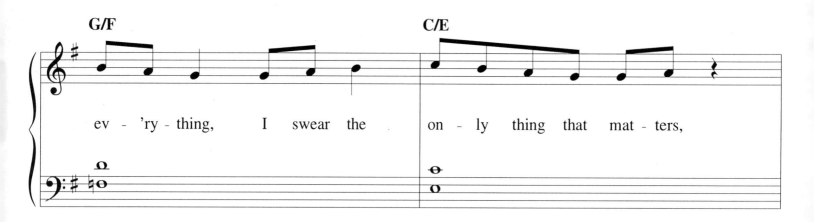

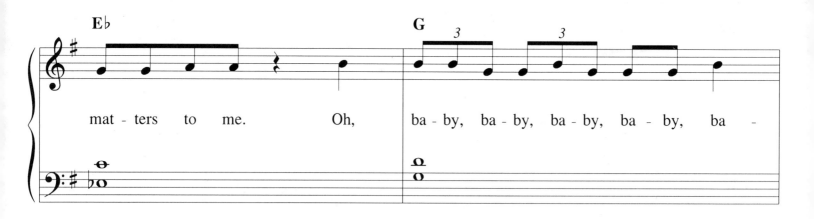